PLANET WHISPERS

Wisdom from Soul Travelers
around the World

Edited by Sophia Fairchild

FOREWORD BY CINDY EYLER

SOUL WINGS® PRESS
Sydney, Australia
Laguna Beach, CA, USA

The authors of this book do not dispense medical advice or prescribe the use of any technique as a form of treatment for physical or medical problems without the advice of a physician, either directly or indirectly. The intent of the editor and authors is only to offer information of a general nature to help you in your quest for emotional and spiritual well-being. In the event you use any of the information in this book for yourself, which is your personal right, the authors, editor and the publisher assume no responsibility for your actions.

Soul Wings® Oracle quotes printed with permission from the author and Soul Wings® Press. Copyright © 2011 by Sophia Fairchild.

Editorial Supervision by Sophia Fairchild
Book Design by Fiona Raven

Library of Congress Cataloging-in-Publication data
Planet whispers : wisdom from soul travelers around the world / edited by Sophia Fairchild ; foreword by Cindy Eyler.
p. cm.

ISBN 978-0-9845-9305-7
ISBN 978-0-9845-9306-4 (e-book)

1. Self-actualization (Psychology). 2. Spiritual life—Anecdotes. 3. Spirituality. 4. Travel. 5. Travel—Psychological aspects. I. Eyler, Cindy. II. Title.
BF637.P36 F35 2011   158.1 21—DC22   2011910105

ISBN-13 978-0-9845-9305-7
ISBN-10 0-9845-9305-5
DIGITAL ISBN: 978-0-9845-9306-4

First Printing December 2011
Printed in the United States of America

This book is dedicated
to the ancestors of the land,
which gives life to us all,
in helping us share our stories.

Contents

"If you love Travel and Culture, and a touch of Soul Journeys, this is a delightful book to keep you company on cold evenings. *Planet Whispers: Wisdom from Soul Travelers Around the World* is a poignant collection of milestone markers, measuring the distance souls have traveled on Earth through laughter and tears. The layers of truths revealed with every step taken on life's path are portals of appreciation for the surprising blessings the Universe presents in disguise.

The authors of these beautiful stories remind us to have courage as we embark on our own sacred journeys. In the end, our quest to bridge understanding between cultures, to forgive our past, and to honor ourselves and our ancestry all lead us to living our life purpose to the full. May *Planet Whispers* help you find clear answers to your quest."

—GINA ALZATE, Spiritual Warrior, Broadcaster,
Educator & Travel Consultant
www.worldtoursandcruises.com

"Each of the stories in this anthology is such a gift. While I love to travel, I realized that by reading each chapter in *Planet Whispers*, I learned about other societies throughout the world and their various spiritual practices directly from the comfort of my armchair! It is abundantly clear that each author holds a reverence for all that is sacred in this life. I encourage you to take the time to savor their stories, for you will never be the same again!"

—LAURIE BRYAN LARSON, Certified Soul Coach
www.pathways-soulcoaching.com

"*Planet Whispers* is a profound compilation of experiences and awakenings that ordinary people have journeyed through as they remembered and reconnected to the Earth and all her wisdom. Each story in this book allows you to feel that one moment, that one breath, that one heartbeat where these people's reconnections were made and how that changed everything in their lives.

As I read the stories, I felt that I would love to share a meal with these authors, to listen to their voices recount their experiences, to watch the light in their eyes come to life in the retelling, to feel their hearts fill with joy, to share that expansion of energy when we finally connect to the truth of our journey. To honor this Earth is to honor ourselves; to love this Earth is to love ourselves; to respect this Earth is to respect ourselves. Enjoy the wonder in these stories. There is much to remember, and to learn."

—RAELENE BYRNE, Author, Energy Healer, Tour Guide for the Soul
www.medicineforyourspirit.com

Foreword

I was never one of those people that we hear so many times saying: "I've always wanted to go to Egypt!" or: "My biggest dream is to see the pyramids!" Going to Egypt was never on my radar growing up, or even well into adulthood. I knew of the pyramids, but never thought for a moment about them. Yet my life was about to change when I took my first group of travelers on a spiritual journey through Egypt.

I didn't know at the time that this was a deep calling of my soul that was ready for me to experience a huge leap in my personal growth, through re-connecting me to a part of my soul consciousness that I was unaware of. This would be an unlocking of ancient wisdom, knowledge and memories I had already experienced in several past lives in Egypt, both in spirit and in the physical manifestations of "life". I was being beckoned to unite my soul with the Spirit of Egypt to allow an unfolding of greater realizations of who I am, and how my connection with Egypt would become important in the next phase of my life.

In this book, this particular experience would be considered an example of *Planet Whispers*.

> *We are not human beings having a spiritual experience.*
> *We are spiritual beings having a human experience.*
>
> —TEILHARD DE CHARDIN

We are all eternal beings. Eternal meaning: we never really die. We are everlasting beings, souls. Our soul continues to live eternally in all directions of time and space; we are infinite. Our soul is the true essence of who we are, the constant part of our existence, regardless of where we are residing in the Universe (past, present or future, physical or non-physical) at any given time.

Our soul is always awake and always experiencing, whether we are physically awake or asleep, having a physical experience as a human (often referred to as *life*), or living in the technicolor of our Divine heavenly-selves (often referred to as the *after-life*.)

With each lifetime on Planet Earth – past, present or future, or perhaps lives lived on other planets, stars, Universes, or living our true soul-essence in the heavenly-dimensions of the Spirit world – our souls are ever growing and evolving. Wherever you've been, whoever you've been, whatever you've done, seen and experienced, contributes to soul consciousness. The eternal soul is made up of wisdom, knowledge and experiences that we pick up as we soul travel through our soul's paths, whether it is through our spirit or in human form, as we answer our *Planet Whispers*.

I am learning and reflecting on the concept of soul consciousness in real-time as I walk my current soul journey on Planet Earth. To fathom the thought of our soul incarnating lifetime after lifetime in a physical form and beyond, to existences dwelling in Spirit form, can be a wonderful exercise in expanding our awareness. Yet even as I ponder this concept, I know I can only grasp a minute part of it, and that where I am right now is exactly where I'm supposed be on my path of learning and understanding.

I am realizing that the important, soul-touching experiences in my life over the last 15 years of soul travels are things that I never gave a second thought to during most of my earlier life. Now, I could never imagine living without them. At the perfect time and space in my life, I am re-engaged with powerful past life wisdom that enhances my path and rocks my world in amazing ways in absolute perfect divine timing. This is what happens every time I reconnect with Egypt. Definitely loud *Planet Whispers*!

The first year I was guided to lead a spiritual group journey through Egypt, I thought it was a one-time visit before moving on to the next guided destination. Was I ever wrong! After I led that first journey, I soon found myself contacting our guide in Egypt to set up another transformational journey… and each year, another and another! Now it is one of my favorite transformational journey offerings each year.

Through my many journeys in Egypt I have re-ignited my soul connection with the Spirit of Egypt. Together our spirits sing with a passion and love that feels pretty close to Godliness. It was as if I'd lost touch while my soul went off to experience other things to prepare for our reunion. But now that we've been reunited, we vibrate in pure love and joy, celebrating the profound part of our divine essences united as One. I completely embrace the spirit unifications, spiritual knowledge and memories of this country, along with its history, ancient spiritual healing, learning and awareness. There is no denying that these connections are deeply rooted.

It is not uncommon for participants who are guided to make soul journeys to places such as Egypt to experience a deeply transformational shift in all aspects of their personal lives.

Through immersion in such cultures, both ancient and modern, travelers discover so much about their human and soul-selves. For example, when we travel to the Great Pyramid of Giza, the Isis Temple on the Island of Philae, the Temples of Abu Simbel or trek to the top of the vortex of Mt. Sinai, we receive soul information and experience deep connection with our soul's journey. This can enhance our spiritual awareness of our life purpose, and uncover feelings of empowerment, self worth, love and compassion for self and others, and so much more.

Such journeys become an acceleration in one's ascension process and a rare discovery of who we are at deep levels. Through accessing the deepest parts of our soul and reconnecting with knowledge and wisdom, by working with the energies of sacred destinations such as Egypt, soul travelers find clarity, focus, rejuvenation and motivation to live the life of their dreams! The benefits of these soul sojourns can benefit people's lives more than they ever imagined.

Outer Adventure for Inner Discovery through spiritual journeys, or as it is known within the pages of this book, *Planet Whispers*, have proven to be the fastest and most effective way to shift from simply living everyday life to making that breakthrough of living your life with purpose and passion – allowing yourself to hear your own *Planet Whispers* for personal growth and transformation.

In this very special book, you will be amazed at the variety of ways the authors have shared their personal life-changing *Planet Whispers*. For some, it was through visiting a sacred site such as Machu Picchu in Peru, while for others it was being in a common place or connecting with a simple object or piece of jewelry. For another, it was feeling a push to go to a destination without really knowing exactly why, to find himself experiencing a profound vision quest in the isolation and solitude of the Yukon, in the Canadian wilderness. His *Planet Whispers* transformed him from an over-worked, career-driven professional to a person with a renewed passion for spirituality, which in turn enhanced his career path.

There are always *Planet Whispers* speaking to us, nudging us and guiding us to experience life-enhancing transformations. Those who are brave enough to follow their *Planet Whispers* find themselves opening up to lives that are receptive to wonder and joyful enlightenment!

As you enjoy reading these captivating stories of real life people sharing thought-provoking inspiration and insight, perhaps you too will begin to recognize your own *Planet Whispers*.

Life just keeps getting better as we allow our *Planet Whispers* to guide us to our next greatest level!

CINDY EYLER
San Leandro, California

Introduction

Look deep into nature, and then you will understand everything better.

—ALBERT EINSTEIN

*W*hat do we mean by *Planet Earth,* and is it really whispering to us? The word *Planet* comes from a Greek word meaning "wanderer" used to describe the movement of stars. *Earth* comes from an Old English word for the planet on which we live. *Eorthe, Tierra, Terra Mater, Gaia, Pachamama, Papatuānuku, Earth Mother* – no matter what name you choose to call our home, Planet Earth is a blue-green celestial body spinning through space around a golden sun. To many people however, it also has a living presence. For them, the cultivation of a relationship with the Spirit of our planet is an essential part of their daily lives.

In my own life, growing up barefoot around Australian aboriginal people who frequently disappeared into the wild bush country on 'walkabout', I learned by listening to their stories from an early age – something that all indigenous peoples have known for millennia. By trusting in the messages received from the Spirit within nature, all of our needs are catered for, from survival in any wilderness landscape, to a deep sense of belonging and spiritual connection with the land itself.

Seasonal ceremonies practiced by our ancestors, no matter which country they lived in, remind us that we are not just physical beings living in a material world, but that life on this planet also has a spiritual dimension. From the beginning of time, our sense of wholeness as human beings has involved a totality which unites spirit and matter, the human soul and the soul of the earth.

It was the Spirit living within matter which sparked our ancestors' awareness of how all of the diverse parts of life exist in mutually supportive patterns of relationship. This interconnectedness between every living thing continues to sustain the eternal web of life, and allowed our ancestors to live in co-creative harmony with all life on Planet Earth.

The bright soul of the world, the *anima mundi,* has since ancient times been honored as the life-giving, divine principle within creation. It is this spiritual essence within the planet that is still asking to be heard. At the same time, the soul of humanity yearns for reconnection, so that life on earth can once more become sacred.

The late mythologist Joseph Campbell once said that while many so-called *primitive* societies regard nature as something marvelous and miraculous, indeed a manifestation of the divine, our more modern view of the world has cut us off from nature and the sanctity of our own land, so that it no longer appears to speak to us of the divine.

Campbell said that this way of thinking has led us on pilgrimages to distant places we consider more holy, when we already have the potential to hold an awareness of the sacred in this present moment, on the very land where we now sit.

C. G. Jung believed that for our ancestors, the country they inhabited was also the landscape of their soul, which spoke to them in useful ways, helping them to find physical, social and spiritual nourishment.

In addition, he said that without our connection with the earth, we lose our natural instincts, living more and more 'in our head' through our ego, which leads us to feelings of isolation, alienation and disorientation, and to living what feels like a soulless, meaningless life.

The author Laurens van der Post believed that the psychic price we pay for being spiritually out of touch with nature is "a staggering loss of identity and meaning... a kind of loneliness, an inadequate comprehension of what life can be."

When we feel ourselves at odds with the Spirit of the Earth, it's easy to imagine that nature is somehow against us. Yet our ancestors knew that nature was not being unfriendly in times of poor seasons or inclement weather. Rather, they understood that they themselves needed to amend their alliance with nature, and to learn how to better live in harmony with her.

Anyone alive today on this planet will have noticed that it's been a long time since modern society has considered our Earth as sacred, and that we are now living in a world where there is a deep split between spirit and matter.

Beyond the obvious concerns for the state of our environment, this has led us to experience vague feelings of restlessness and dissatisfaction, a feeling that something important is missing from life, and a deep longing for change, for something to be resolved or healed.

But this vital link between the soul of the world and the human soul can indeed be renewed, when we return to the practice of listening for the soft whispers of the planet, as our ancestors once did.

Our sense of separation and woundedness can also be healed when we forgive ourselves for forgetting our timeless human relationship with the Spirit of the living Earth, and listen again with our hearts.

As we heal the divisions between the human and planetary soul; as these two worlds are actively reunited and reborn within our own hearts, we ourselves are healed. We are then able to see the world with fresh eyes, and our passion for the wonder and magic of life is restored.

The resulting change in the way we then approach living on this planet holds within it the potential not only for deep inner peace, but the assured mutual futures of both humanity and Mother Earth.

Our ancestors knew how to receive whispered messages from the planet by noticing the movements of animals, birds and fish, and through watching for patterns in the wind, sea and sky. They also followed the guidance provided by nature in their dreams, often in the form of whispered messages from the spirits of birds, animals, rivers and trees.

In spite of much evidence to the contrary, people living in the modern, urban world have not lost the deep wisdom of their instincts, nor have they lost the ability to cultivate a collaborative relationship with the natural world. This is demonstrated in the joy and appreciation felt by city dwellers for even the smallest of gardens tucked away beneath forests of skyscrapers.

Though our natural instincts may be lying dormant within many of us, as long as we refrain from a pathological urge to dominate nature, and begin to work with her instead, we are all still fully capable of hearing the whispers of the planet at any time.

All it takes is to allow ourselves to listen more deeply.

We too can see the landscape of our own soul reflected back to us in the beauty and magic of the landscapes all around us. Through discovering and interacting with our own sacred sites, even in our own neighborhoods, these special places will in turn begin to recognize and respond to us.

When we truly connect with the roots of our own consciousness, deeply embedded within the soul of the planet, going beyond simply consuming nature's gifts, we too will receive the same spiritual nourishment from the land that our ancestors once did.

In this book, you will travel with professional Soul Guides and Spiritual Practitioners from all over the world, exploring new terrain and techniques that will help you experience the deep peace and timeless wisdom within the heart of our planet.

The personal experiences shared here reveal a variety of ways to forge a rich relationship with nature's wisdom, opening us up to an active communication with the living world we all share.

The stories speak for themselves. Each illustrates a different path taken by an individual author to reconnect with the soul of the world, enlivening their own soul in the process. Each journey is also an inner voyage from the head to the heart, to reawaken with clarity to the deeper potentials within their own lives.

These diverse and thought provoking stories demonstrate how the Earth is whispering to all of us in many different ways. Some seek solace in the silence of the wilderness to hear her speak, while others journey to sacred sites. Many discover signs and messages that expand and enrich their spiritual life right in their own back yard.

Nature is always whispering her teachings to us. Through deep listening, with both our inner and outer ears, we can learn to live these teachings with wisdom and balance, and in the process, inspire, heal and uplift our own lives and the lives of those we touch.

By sharing theses stories, the authors of this book hope that your own path of communication will be reawakened as you read them, so that you too will hear the whispers of the planet.

May these stories speak to your heart. And may your journey through *Planet Whispers* help you discover the power of these whispered messages to deeply nourish and refresh your soul.

SOPHIA FAIRCHILD
Sydney, Australia

Expectation

I set my course with confidence.

The wind, full of inspiration and insight, blows change in our direction, empowering us to initiate necessary life changes. As we prepare for the journey ahead, optimism and a joyful heart are the most important resources to take with us.

RAYMOND TORRENTI
Pittsfield, Massachusetts, USA

RAYMOND TORRENTI is a writer, teacher, healer, and certified Soul Coach. He has dedicated his life to exploring spirituality, mysticism, shamanism, healing and psychic phenomena. In the process he has met indigenous healers and spiritual teachers from around the world. He has directed spirituality programs for health care organizations and educational institutions, lectured at universities and conferences, led workshops and retreats, and provided consultation to professionals. His 2003 book, *Analyzing the Transcendent: Psychotherapists and Their Mystical Experiences*, examined the mystical experiences of psychotherapists and how those experiences affected their personal and professional lives.

Raymond now lives in a cottage on a lake in the Berkshires of Massachusetts where he remains close to nature and enjoys the outdoors. Bicycling, swimming, and kayaking are his favorite activities. He writes and works with people, both individually and in groups, in the area of personal and spiritual development. As a soul coach, he weaves together his knowledge of psychology and spirituality – along with his gifts as a mystic and intuitive – to assist each person to discover their authentic self and live an intentional and enlightened life.

Raymond holds a Ph.D. in psychology and spirituality from the University Professors Program at Boston University, a Master of Divinity degree from the Weston School of Theology in Cambridge, Massachusetts, and a Bachelor of Arts in Biblical Studies and American Studies from Barrington College in Rhode Island. He is a National Certified Counselor and Licensed Mental Health Counselor in Massachusetts.

www.raymondtorrenti.com

Vision Quest at the Arctic Circle

RAYMOND TORRENTI, PhD

For better or worse I was going to the Yukon.

$\mathscr{L}$ooking back over the spiritual experiences I have had during my life, the journey to the Yukon Territory was one of the most significant. This place was remote, to say the least, yet the spiritual experience I had there remains with me to this day.

Having completed my doctoral degree in psychology and spirituality at Boston University the year before, my life now seemed directionless and empty. For eight years I was engulfed with intense academic studies, clinical training and qualifying exams, culminating with the writing and defense of a dissertation. At that time, I worked three jobs to support myself and pay for tuition. Everything in my life was oriented toward completing the doctoral requirements and graduation.

With a new identity as 'doctor' and clinical credentials for a promising future, I felt uncertain about what I really wanted for a career. After years accommodating myself to the demands of professors and fulfilling requirements, I had lost touch with my desires. Three jobs supported me, but now they felt empty and had no meaning.

My decision to go to the Yukon Territory was made in the first months of 1996. I received a Christmas letter from my old friend, Jim, from theology school. We had graduated from a Master of Divinity program and he was ordained as a priest. Now he was assigned to a parish in Dawson City in the Yukon Territory. Every year I received a Christmas letter telling me how much he loved it there. Living in Boston for many years, this puzzled me. I enjoyed an urban lifestyle and could not imagine being so isolated. That year he invited me to visit him.

I sensed a strange urge to go. Looking at my work schedule, I determined that June was the best month to travel. After some consideration and looking into how I would get there, I decided to make the trip. I also resolved to do a personal retreat and vision quest, hoping to find some answers.

A few days before leaving, I wrote to Jim and expressed some fears. "I am a bit nervous venturing into the unknown. I'm not even sure what to pack or what kind of weather to expect. Anyway, I will pack light and will be adaptable."

Pilgrimage to the Yukon Territory

Modern pilgrimages are different from ancient ones – walking long distances, enduring the weather and the risk of bandits. I faced airport security, passport checks and blaring monitors with news, commercials and flight information, yet despite this technical aspect of modern travel, I was on an ancient quest, a spiritual pilgrimage.

Pilgrimage. The word evokes traveling to sacred places like churches, temples and shrines. Yet for me the entire planet is sacred. The Yukon Territory was one of the few places still untouched by civilization. I let go of my familiar routine and schedule. I left family, friends and colleagues behind. With the desire to shed the years of accumulated burnout from my academic years, I chose to escape into the unknown and unfamiliar, hoping to find meaning and purpose.

It was a long trip from Boston to Vancouver to Whitehorse to Dawson City. While boarding the small jet for Whitehorse, I experienced fear and I questioned what I was doing. Was this a crazy idea? I worried that nothing would happen, whether I would come back feeling worse. An urge to abandon the trip came over me. Then the plane moved on the runway, built up power and launched into the sky. For better or worse I was going to the Yukon.

As we flew over the mountains with clouds circling the peaks, rays of sunshine moved like spotlight beams beneath them. It gave me the impression I was being guided forward and was going in the right direction. Yet I still felt fear of facing the unknown.

I arrived in Whitehorse about 10:00 p.m. Fortunately, Jim was waiting in the airport and greeted me along with his dog, Sammy. Seeing him, I recalled his good nature and humor and felt less afraid. We stayed at a local rectory before traveling on to Dawson City. I was tired and went to my room. I had to close the windows with thick, dark green shades to keep out the sunlight, but the quiet helped me to fall asleep.

The next morning we prepared for the six-hour drive to Dawson City. Jim had an old red truck. The windshield was cracked from the impact of small stones, and extra tires were stowed in the back because the rough logging roads caused frequent flat tires. There was nothing except tall trees lining the road all the way to Dawson, allowing us plenty of time to talk and catch up on each other's lives.

Finding our Natural Rhythm

I move through life with pleasure and balance.

Too much work creates imbalance. Yet the earth already turns on our behalf. All we need do is align with its natural rhythms. Be still, watch for the signs, determine the path, then move forward with ease. By finding our natural rhythm, all work becomes meaningful, the blessing of joy in action.

After stopping once for a flat tire, we finally arrived. Dawson City looked like an old western town from a cowboy movie, with dirt roads, wooden buildings and even a saloon. The mountains behind the town were stunning. This was my base camp for the trip.

Since the Summer Solstice was the next day, I asked Jim if we could find a place to observe this special occasion. I thought it would be a good way to begin my spiritual retreat. Jim thought the best place to go was the Arctic Circle. So the next day we left Dawson City for another six-hour drive to Eagle Plain, on the Arctic Circle. We packed the truck, brought extra gas and drove north. It was another long trip on logging roads with nothing but vast treeless plains and high mountains.

Eagle Plain reminded me of a small rest stop on a highway. We booked rooms for the night at the only hotel and ate a meal in the diner. The woman taking our order had to check to see if they still had items on the menu since the supply truck had not yet arrived, and food was limited. Without a doubt, this was the most remote place I had ever been.

Summer Solstice at Eagle Plain on the Arctic Circle
June 21, 1996
At 7:24 p.m., on top of a mountain near Eagle Plain at the Arctic Circle, I celebrated the Summer Solstice. It was sunny and still. I meditated for a few hours, attempting to harmonize myself with the energy around me during this special time. There was such a gentle, soft energy in this place. I took in the stillness and peace of this sacred moment.

There was daylight the entire day. I watched the sun traveling in a great circle – never setting. This was so foreign to me; it was as though I was on another planet. Solstices mark the end and the beginning of a cycle. This was why I came here – to mark the end of a chapter in my life so that I could move into something new. In meditation, I realized the significance of this moment. It was a spiritual death. It was time to die to old patterns and give birth to new ones.

Death is about letting go. I could only hope that a new vision would emerge. I longed to re-establish a connection with my authentic self and truly discover what I wanted for my professional future. I did not know what I would discover and had to be prepared for the possibility that nothing would happen. There could be no expectations. I needed to sit, be still and be receptive. The only certainty was that I had made a bold and radical move to be in the presence of the Creator.

It was very still during the Solstice. I breathed in the quiet, taking in the energy. To mark this occasion, I wanted to make some kind of offering. With nothing around to create an offering ceremony, I sat and expressed my intentions through simple prayer. I always sensed the Creator guiding me to get a doctorate. This degree was the most important accomplishment of my life and the fulfillment of a dream. Now I wanted to offer it as a gift to the Creator, seeking how to best use this education and training to serve others. By making this offering, I was returning my accomplishments to the Creator.

In this holy moment, I also made an offering of prayer for the people who supported me along the way. I held each in my heart and spoke their names, releasing them into the sky on this strange, sunny night. I prayed for their spiritual journeys and blessed each of them with peace.

After making my prayer offerings, I watched for a response, a sign. I sat and waited. There was nothing – just stillness and silence. It was getting late, and I needed to end my meditation. Although nothing overtly happened, I felt my offerings were received and that this was enough for now.

Retreat
June 22–24, 1996
After the Solstice, I retreated to Dome Mountain just outside of Dawson City for three days. During this time, I either walked or sat for most of each day. Though unintended at the time, it turned into a process of interior purification. My restlessness gradually settled down. The sun made its circular orbit in the sky, the animals and birds followed their simple daily routines, and the mountains stood as they had long before I was born. I began to hear sounds I had not paid attention to before and saw things that had eluded my vision.

Being immersed in nature slowed my thinking enough to become aware of the primal rhythm and ease of everyday life, which seemed to poke fun at the hectic urban lifestyle I had been living back in Boston. All my ambitions seemed meaningless here. Nature went on, with or without me, and put my personal strivings into perspective.

Out of this immersion came a growing awareness of how small my identity was compared to the expanse of nature and the cosmos. All my attempts to make a meaningful life from credentials and outside accomplishments created a kind of artificial self, and I lived it like an actor playing a scene. I got so lost in this created self that I lost contact with my authentic self – my soul.

Being in nature was cleansing me of this created identity. It was a slow, gradual process that required me to remain still and attentive to the present moment. This purification was vital. It took the shedding of layer after layer of this artificial self before I could sense a path to my authentic self.

Walking around the top of Dome Mountain, I looked out at the endless landscape and saw Dawson City below next to a river. I began to feel part of nature instead of feeling like an alien visitor. By the time these three days were completed, I was ready to go deeper and take the risk of a vision quest. When I returned to the house where I was staying, I asked Jim if I could borrow his truck and if he could recommend somewhere in the area for a vision quest. He suggested going north to an area known as Tombstone (in 1999 it was officially designated as Tombstone Territorial Park). It was a wilderness, and he said I would find the isolation and solitude I was seeking in these mountains. Even the name Tombstone was a sign to me that this was the right place since I sought spiritual death and resurrection.

I prepared that evening by packing some provisions in case of an emergency and made an arrangement with Jim that if I did not return after a period of time, he would come and find me. I left early in the morning, taking the logging roads we used to head toward Eagle Plain, then followed the route Jim had given me to enter the wilderness of Tombstone.

Vision Quest at Tombstone Mountain
June 25, 1996

I arrived at the base of Tombstone Mountain and parked the truck. Everything seemed to come to a sudden halt. I left the truck with my walking stick, and looking up, found a place to begin my trek toward the peak. The terrain was otherworldly with grey jagged rocks and bits of low scrub here and there. I was surprised by how easy it was to climb on and over the rocks once I got my balance. It took some time to get close to the peak.

The rhythm of my footsteps was the only sound I could hear as I moved upward brushing past scrub and rocks. Both frightening and exciting, I realized I was over one hundred miles from the nearest person. There were no cars, no airplanes overhead, and no other noises that make up ordinary modern life. The isolation was the most extreme I had ever experienced in my life.

Close to the peak I found a relatively flat area of rocks and dirt. It looked like a great place to sit. I took my walking stick and drew a large circle in the dirt around me. Looking out at the landscape, I made an agreement with myself not to leave this circle and just be receptive to the Creator. I trusted that somehow I would know when it was time to leave.

With no watch or other timepiece, I entered a timeless moment made even more disorienting by the constant sun in the sky. It followed an elliptical path and at it lowest point, made the day seem like dusk. Disengaging from time, I truly entered a kind of void where all reference points vanish.

I sat and became aware of the deafening silence. This silence was so intense that it was as if I had lost my hearing and was enclosed in a very small space, even though I was in a seemingly endless wilderness. Then there was a sound. It was hard to know where it was coming from. I looked all around trying to see the source of it. It was low and steady and made me a bit afraid. The environment was so still, with not even a breeze to stir the air. It was as if the universe had suddenly stopped. Then I realized where the sound was coming from – it was coming from me. I was amazed that the sound of my own heart beating seemed so foreign to me, and I marveled at how loudly it broke through the absolute silence.

During this moment, I felt one with the cosmos and understood in a new way an ancient Christian notion of the Sacred Heart – not of Jesus, but the Sacred Heart of the Creator beating infinitely for eternity. I became aware that this Sacred

Heart is beating all the time and is the foundation of all existence. I began to cry because simultaneously I realized my own beating heart was a manifestation of the Sacred Heart, and we were beating in rhythm, beating in harmony with each other. I cried over the Creator's compassion for me, that the Divine Source was bonding with me through our hearts. Now I understood this ancient notion more deeply because I realized all hearts beat in harmony and are manifestations of the Sacred Heart.

Then my awareness seemed to gradually expand. I took in the area around me – the rocks, the scrub, the mountain, the wilderness, the sky, and the sun – and all these fragments came together as one. Being this far north on the planet gave me a perspective I would not have had anywhere else on earth. For as the sun circled in the sky, I could see in a poetic way that the planet was tilting or bowing to its source, the sun. The earth travels in orbit around the sun and when it tilts to the sun, it is in alignment with it – there is light, day and night.

This poetic vision from nature mirrored back to me a profound awakening of why I came here to do a vision quest. By traveling this far north on the planet, I was, in some sense, coming here to tilt or bow to my Divine Source. This long journey was about aligning myself to my soul and the Divine Source. In bowing to my soul and the Creator, I experienced enlightenment about my purpose. It was to allow my authentic self to shine in the world by remaining at one with my soul and by letting Divine Light guide me along the way. I did not need a directive to 'do' something – I needed a process of living an authentic life that would create my future. What a tremendous insight I had received from the Creator.

The Return

I do not know how long this experience lasted, but at some point it was complete. Before breaking circle, I took some time to reflect on what had happened. The experience did not bring a new directive the way I thought it might. It brought a profound enlightenment that all my efforts – the academic accomplishments, degrees, professional training, efforts at self-development, and the relationships in my life – were all part of a greater mysterious cosmic dance that was unfolding as it should, and just being part of it was enough. I did not have to 'do' anything more than simply stay connected with my soul and let my authentic self shine fully in the world.

This new awareness was a wonderful relief. With no pressure to 'do' anything, I suddenly was free, and it unblocked the path to my soul. This freedom permitted me to listen to my inner desires and let go of all the expectations others had of me. Credentials did not determine my identity. My life path was determined by expressing my deepest longings and passions. My future career would be shaped by my soul's desires, and the deepest passion had always been the area of spirituality. Now I understood that whatever direction my career took, spirituality would be central and would guide me along the way.

After I broke circle, I began to descend the mountain. Part of me wanted to stay because the experience was so sublime. Yet that sacred moment had passed, and I knew I could not re-enter it. Gradually I arrived at the old red truck at the bottom of the mountain. It was difficult driving back and entering ordinary life again. I was thankful I had some hours of traveling to adjust.

Conclusion

Traveling to the Arctic Circle for a vision quest is a rare opportunity. I was grateful to have had the chance to visit this beautiful territory and was deeply appreciative for the spiritual experience I had there. After returning to Boston, I dropped one of my three jobs and began simplifying and redirecting my life. I listened to my soul and started to incorporate my passion for spirituality into my career path.

Silence, stillness, and solitude are deep gifts in life. With all the high tech distractions, non-stop information and social communications that fill our world, these gifts become ever more precious. It takes effort, but it is possible to cultivate these gifts in our lives, whether at home, in a park, or traveling the world.

My bond with nature continues to be important, and a few years ago I finally moved out of Boston. Now I live in a rural area, rich with natural surroundings, where I can immerse myself in nature as I did in the Yukon. Watching the change of seasons, the stars at night, the forests, the lakes, the animals and birds – reminds me of my oneness with the world. The Divine Heart beats everywhere and the Divine Light shines in each soul. When I am silent and alone, I find myself reconnecting with my Yukon experience and remembering the importance of offerings, my authentic self, and that I am part of a great and mysterious cosmos.

Earth Offering Ceremony

A few years after traveling to the Yukon, I went to Peru and Bolivia to study indigenous healing practices. While there, I came across a sacred practice known as an Earth Offering – a ceremony that allows you to return gifts back to the Creator. This indigenous practice is steeped in ancient tradition foreign to us; however I have distilled the essence of the ceremony into its three core steps.

A) Preparing the Earth Offering

In preparation you will need a few materials. First, select a piece of paper that is about two feet by two feet. I prefer tissue or wrapping paper since it folds easily. Then gather two strings or pieces of twine, each about three feet in length.

You will then need to assemble some ingredients. You can use any of those I mention below, or you can be creative and come up with your own. It is important to think about what these ingredients will represent for you. Those I often use are:

1. Bay or Sage leaves (for the intention)
2. Seeds (beginnings)
3. Rice (abundance)

4. Cornmeal or Tobacco (gratitude)
5. Salt (protection)
6. Incense grains (purification)
7. Confetti paper (joy)
8. Sugar or candy (sweetness)
9. Essential oils or cologne (release)
10. Some paper and a pen (for your prayer)

B) Creating the Earth Offering
1. Open the ceremony with a prayer and articulate the intention of the offering.
2. Lay the strings on the ground, one vertical and one horizontal, crossing in the middle.
3. Lay the paper over the strings.
4. Hold some Bay or Sage leaves; gently blow your intention on the leaves, and place them in the center of the paper to anchor the intention.
5. Then take one of the ingredients, hold it in your hand, and with prayer and compassion infuse the ingredient with the energy of your intention by gently blowing on it.
6. Place the ingredient on the paper in whatever pattern you feel led to design.
7. Repeat steps 5 and 6 until all the ingredients are used or until all intentions are fully expressed on the paper. If in a group, let each person select an ingredient, follow steps 5 and 6, and create a group offering.
8. On a separate piece of paper, write down your prayer for this offering, fold the paper, and place it in the center over the leaves. If in a group, each person should write and place their written prayers one at a time.
9. A final blessing is spoken over the offering and if anything needs to be said to complete the ceremony it can be done at this time.
10. In a reverent manner, fold the paper into a small, square bundle and tie it with the strings.
11. You can seal the bundle by placing Bay or Sage leaves under the knot or by sealing the knot with some melted wax.
12. The bundle is now ready to be released.

C) Releasing the Earth Offering
There are three ways of releasing the Earth Offering. You can burn it, bury it, or offer it in a body of water. Each way represents something different: burning indicates you are ready to release something that no longer serves you – transforming it into smoke that rises to the heavens (it is suggested that you turn your back on it as it burns to indicate you are not looking back); burying signifies that you are seeding your intention so that it will manifest in the future; and placing the bundle in a body of water indicates you have achieved some accomplishment or received a gift and are offering it to the water to carry it on for greater good in the world.

These steps of the Earth Offering can take place indoors or outdoors. Keep in mind when and where you will create and release the bundle so that the ceremony will unfold without interruption. It is fine if some time passes between creating the Earth Offering and releasing it, until a fire, burial place, or body of water becomes available. In this case, the bundle should be kept in a sacred place in your home and not disturbed until you are able to release it.

Once the ceremony is complete, your offering is given back to the Creator.

∾

Bibliography

Abram, David. *The Spell of the Sensuous: Perception and Language in a More-Than-Human World.* 1st ed. New York: Pantheon Books, 1996.

Cooper, David A. *Silence, Simplicity, and Solitude: A Guide for Spiritual Retreat.* 1st ed. New York: Bell Tower, 1992.

de Waal, Esther. *To Pause at the Threshold: Reflections on Living on the Border.* North American ed. Harrisburg, Pennsylvania: Morehouse Publishing, 2001.

Linn, Denise, and Meadow Linn. *Quest: Journey to the Centre of Your Soul.* London: Rider, 1997.

Linn, Denise, and Meadow Linn. *Quest: A Guide for Creating Your Own Vision Quest.* 1st Ballantine Books trade ed. New York: Ballantine, 1999.

Magee, Matthew, and Oscar Miro-Quesada. *Peruvian Shamanism: The Pachakúti Mesa.* Chelmsford, MA: Middle Field Publications, 2002.

Torrenti, Raymond. *Analyzing the Transcendent: Psychotherapists and Their Mystical Experiences.* Chelmsford, Massachusetts: Middle Field Publications, 2003.

BRONWYN MAKEDA ASET

Sydney, Australia

SINCE BIRTH, BRONWYN has been able to sense and see spirit. When the essential questions of life were not answered by the mundane, she turned her eyes towards the esoteric and so began her journey back to soul. With many twists and turns in the road, Bronwyn relied on intuition and flow to lead her. As a result, she completed a degree in teaching, visual arts and literature. As flow is ever changing, Bronwyn takes the skills learnt from her degree to impart knowledge gained from her divine studies.

Commitment to her path began 5 years ago when Bronwyn discovered her talents could be used for the greater good. Defining herself meant defining her services, resulting in her business, *Soul Gateways*. As a lifelong learner, Bronwyn is continually gaining new expertise in the metaphysical sciences. Currently enrolled at Australian College for Spiritual Development and International College of Healing and Metaphysics, Bronwyn considers knowledge a key tool in understanding wisdom communicated from the soul.

Qualified as a Doreen Virtue Angel Intuitive™ and Liquid Crystal practitioner, Bronwyn takes her clients on a journey to personal self-discovery. Working collaboratively with spirit, Bronwyn provides a transformational experience that allows you to remember who you truly are. This remembrance assists in your everyday experience of life as well as in your relationships with others.

If you would like to undergo a personal transformation consultation with Bronwyn either online, over the phone or in person, please pay a visit to www.soulgateways.com

Valley of Sangomas – The Universal Me

BRONWYN MAKEDA ASET

I was sixteen when I first heard the silent ancestral stirrings in my heart.

I was looking for direction. South Africa had been calling to me, like a silent whisper as I slept. It was a familiar feeling, this yearning to explore the depths of my being, my heritage. My ego told me that I had done all the work, learnt all the lessons that I needed to learn. Yet I still felt that longing.

Being born and raised in Australia had been difficult for me. I never really felt I belonged. Having to go to an Australian school, then coming home to a completely different culture was confusing growing up. I found myself drawn to the first generation Australians. We leaned on each other when our parents wouldn't allow us to integrate with the 'Aussie' way. I was sixteen when I first heard the silent ancestral stirrings in my heart.

My hair had always been chemically straightened. It seemed almost traditional amongst members of my family and other South Africans of mixed blood, a subtle effect of Apartheid. It occurred to me that I had no idea what my natural hair looked like. I longed to know the texture. Would it curl? Would it be afro? Or would it be thick and wavy? I continued on the train that morning, missing the first three periods of school and had my head shaved. Thus began my quest to finding me. Later I realized it was my ancestral spirit consciousness calling. It would call again till the silent whisper became a loud calling and I had no choice but to explore the home of my ancestors.

January 8th, 2010 began with overwhelming anticipation. I looked around the room where I had been staying in Durban, South Africa, with my Aunty Bev, my dad's younger sister, for the last time, making sure I had everything. I had already been in South Africa for six weeks. The culture shock was all-consuming. Experiencing the pain and suffering of so many, including my family, had made me physically ill.

This was a place of amazing beauty, but the way that it had been neglected broke my heart. The lack of respect and pure ignorance of the depth of history, which lies just beneath the surface of the land, left me feeling empty. My journey thus far included exploring the rich heritage of this unique country, from the echoing cries of injustice that rang through the corridors of Robbin Island Prison, to the clockwork stirrings of the Table Mountain vortex. My heart was overwhelmed by the legacy this land bestowed on humanity.

Now, it was my chance to be guided spiritually into the heritage that I claimed. My cousin had arranged a week in the Valley of Sangomas, traditionally known as Mautse Valley, now renamed Rustler's Valley. She said that DNA from every existing tribal culture had been found there. This place was sacred. IsiSangoma (plural) from every tribe in South Africa traveled there to receive their initiation after receiving the calling. The valley itself in the heart of the Drakensburg Mountains was older than time itself.

The *Drakensberg*, meaning the "Dragon Mountains" in Dutch and Afrikaans, and *uKhahlamba*, "barrier of spears" in Zulu, was birthed from volcanic rock 200 million years ago. Magma had spewed through cracks in the earth as Gondwana-land began to break up. This Drakensberg Lava hardened and created solid basalt rock 1400 meters thick, coating the top of the mountain range. Underneath this lay desert sand which hardened to form sandstone. Today, due to erosion, you can see where the lava stops and the sandstone begins, red rock that fades into white. Just thinking of this place sent shivers down my spine and filled me with a sense of awe.

All my bags were now packed; I was headed to the bus station. I would have to take this part of my journey alone, into the unknown. The ticket was a one way to Bethlehem, where a mysterious Sangoma (traditionally a medicine man) would meet me and whisk me off to the Garden of Eden. I chuckled to myself. How ironic! My first stop on the way to my intended transformation was called 'Bethlehem.' It was a sure sign that I was going in the right direction and perhaps even the first step towards birthing my own Christ-self.

His name was Niyan, or Ni Nixiwaka as he had been dubbed. A perfect name for a Sangoma I thought, taking in the scenery through the bus window. As we drove more inland towards the Free State, or my free state, it seemed, I noticed how the landscape changed from flat grassy plains to rolling mountains. These mountains lay randomly scattered like large dragons that had gone to sleep on a wide green lawn, their spear tipped tails curled. Sometimes a leg stuck out, or a wing. Some had spikes on their backs; some were smooth and almost geometrical in shape. They were all alive, waiting for the right time to show themselves, to the right people. I could almost hear them breathe as I concentrated intensely on each one, looking for any sign of movement as the bus passed.

It was only a 6 hour bus ride to my destination. But it seemed like forever as I passed in and out of time, taking myself to other places, imagining who or what would be waiting for me when the bus stopped. I expected an old Zulu man to be waiting there, a Sangoma with unlimited knowledge who could tell me exactly who I was, tell me the truths of the ages as I picked his brain for wisdom, as all my questions were answered one by one...

I got off the bus, dragging my humungous suitcase aside, then anxiously waited for the mystic to teleport me to another world of sacred African tradition, my own tradition. "Bron?" A strange hippy looking white man called out my name. Straight out of the 1960s, he looked like he had just attended Woodstock, with matted almost dreadlocked hair, and a sun-aged face with twinkling eyes. How did this stranger know my name? I held my purse closer to me. I was, after all, in South Africa, alone in the middle of nowhere. I had heard the horrific stories of rape and abduction and wasn't about to become a victim.

Arms outstretched he came towards me and embraced me as I struggled to understand what was happening. "Niyan" he said, telling me his name as he held me tight. I began to feel the love stream from his body and my intuition told me it was alright. He lifted my suitcase, commenting on how heavy it was, into the back of his bakkie, the South African word for ute, or utility vehicle. I couldn't help but stare at him, wondering what HE was going to teach me about my African tribal heritage and how he would connect me to my ancestors. As my ego made judgments, it started to rain, in fact pour down, as if Mother Nature knew exactly what I needed. The water began to cleanse my thoughts and open my mind to the week ahead.

Niyan told me his story as we drove towards his home in the valley. He had been a photographer in amongst the hustle and bustle of Johannesburg, the center of South African business and cosmopolitan lifestyle, a fast paced city, not unlike Sydney, where if you're not careful the rat race pulls you in without so much as a thought. At the height of his career, a fire swept through, taking all that he had – his business, equipment and home. Dazed and confused he got into his car and started to drive and followed his heart until he arrived at the Valley.

Traditionally, in African and Zulu tradition, isiSangoma have a calling, an ancestral cry that overwhelms their very being, which calls them into the wilderness and completely transforms them. It is a summons from the land itself and the people who lived there, to continue on with their traditions and be a bridge between the worlds of spirit. When they return, transformed, they then seek guidance from an Elder Sangoma who has been through the ritual which allows them to teach others, and then begin their journey. This can take years as they go through training and become ready for the ritual and rites that give one the title *Sangoma*.

Niyan explained to me that he began by living off the land. He built himself a mud brick hut and through guidance, became interested in shamanism. He explained to me that he had been trained and initiated in the Brazilian spiritual practices of Santo Daime but found the doctrine restrictive. So now he continued to be taught by a Yawa Bane Huni Kuin Kaxinawa, a Peruvian shaman who he regularly visited for rituals and mentorship.

My head was spinning. All these words and none of them pertaining to any dialect remotely African! How was he going to help me find my ancestors? I took a deep breath and tried to silence my ego which was again trying to form clouds of doubt in my mind. I smiled, shook off the feeling, and continued to listen to details of what my week ahead would entail. There would be sweat lodges, vision quests, drumming, journeying and sacred rituals with set intentions. Suddenly, my week didn't sound too bad. I let go of all my expectations and decided to enjoy the ride.

The sun shone through the cracks in the window awnings as I awoke. I took a deep breath and noticed how it filled my lungs and then moved through my bloodstream through to every inch of my body. It was day two. The night before, I had experienced my first sweat lodge. My intention during the sweat was to open my heart to the journey and quest for knowledge that lay before me. I felt the effects immediately and it seemed that I had been transformed during my sleep, the intentions of the sweat lodge settling in as my mind rested.

I took a walk outside and everything appeared brighter. The blades of grass emitted a subtle light that shone as each blade swayed with the wind. The mountains around me purred a low hum as the clouds above took on shapes that it seemed represented their very individual essence. Everything was alive with being, aware of my presence, but not asking anything of me, just a mutual acknowledgement as I in turn acknowledged them.

I left Niyan as he prepared for our next couple days' ritual and started to walk to the "Eye of the Valley." Not knowing the way, I let my intuition guide me. Consciously tuning into my heart, it wasn't too long before I started singing. A soft hum at first grew into a loud harmonic melody of random words and what seemed to be invocations. As I sang, my feet walked in rhythm. The wind blew in rhythm and in turn everything around me beat in time to my song.

Music had long been a part of my culture and upbringing, however I never thought of myself as musical to say the least. In fact, I often held back when it came to singing, afraid of what judgments would be passed when I opened my mouth. Yet here I was singing music unknown to me on the top of my lungs! I had in fact found one of the songlines pertaining to the Valley. These lines, according to indigenous Australian Aborigines, are paths embedded in the land which assist with navigation.

To access these lines you simply sing the correct melodic tune, feeling the story of the land. Language is not a barrier but the rhythm is key, as well as being in tune with the land itself. Music has for eons been a significant way of connecting to the divine. The earliest pre-historic findings have been of bone carved flutes. It is even thought that the early humans sang before they talked. Evidence of this can be seen in the different indigenous cultures that still remain today. Music plays a big part of their culture and rituals, regardless of continent.

It occurred to me that I was miles away from Australia yet was practicing an Aboriginal ritual that I had no idea about. I was trying to connect to my African heritage and here I was being Australian! The identity line had once again been blurred and I was feeling more confused than ever. The dots just didn't seem to want to connect the way that I had intended.

On the outskirts of the opposing mountains, Niyan and I sat in a cave. It is here that we carried out an Amazonian ritual intended to open your third eye and teach a prescribed lesson of your personal choice. It was day four and I had asked during the ritual for my voice, the voice of my ancestors.

I walked around the cave waiting for the signal to make my way to the waterfall below. Carved into sandstone by the sheer force of water that had long been and gone, the now deserted cave was once the home to the indigenous people of this land. All that now remains are faint etchings of their survival on the cave wall. I placed my ear to the cold sandstone, closed my eyes and waited. Pictures formed in my mind of celebrations, dancing and thanksgiving rituals. The people were truly one with this cave and the land within which they dwelled. Niyan signaled that it was time to go. The bubbling sound of water called out to me as I crossed the sandy landscape of the cave to the lush, alive-green forest. As I walked through it, the elementals peeked out from behind their trees, curious to see who this new energy in their forest was, and what I might want.

With every step, I felt I was approaching something big. Then, like a mirage forming in front of my eyes, the forest gave way to beautiful rock formations which supported a seemingly infinitive waterfall. With no beginning and an unknown end, the water poured forth with enormous power, shooting out from an undetermined source. I felt at ease and nurtured. This place emitted a definitive feminine energy. I explored the surrounding area until I found a rock that was strangely familiar. I sat down and lay on the rock, my body molded into the surface below me as if Mother Nature knew I was coming and intentionally prepared this rock for my exact figure. I let my head fall back and closed my eyes, taking in the sounds around me.

All of a sudden, I felt a movement around my base chakra. I focused my intention on that part of my body. There lay two coiled snakes, one dark blue and the other light. As my awareness became known, they started to shift, curling their way up my body until they reached my throat chakra. Violently they started ripping at my throat. Numb to the experience, not knowing whether or not to feel scared or sick or grateful, I just lay there and allowed them to tear chunks of past blockages out from my throat. A sticky like black goo dripped from their fangs and I thought about the years of conditioning stuck there, holding me back from who I truly was. Suddenly they stopped and retreated from whence they came. A surge of peace overwhelmed my body, a sense that I had never experienced before. But it was more than peace; it was love, unconditional love that came from within me but also from without.

The rock which was so perfectly carved to fit my body became me. The waterfall and her feminine nurturing was mine. "I" in fact was no longer there and Bronwyn only existed as love. Even though I had in the past, touched on this part of me; it was for only a fleeting moment, a mere glimpse of what I truly was. Here and now it was not the past me or the future of who I was to become, but simply me. I opened my eyes and felt nature around me and realized for the first time what all those books that I had read that talked about oneness really meant.

As I lay there, content with my being, the clouds moved and covered the sun.

After a while I started to feel cold though not uncomfortable. The sprays of the waterfall in the shade had lowered my body temperature. I looked to the sky and, as if it was not even a question that my thoughts would not be heard or my request carried out, I politely asked them to move so the sun could once again warm my body. Without hesitation, the clouds acknowledged and shifted. After a while I felt hot, so I asked the clouds again to shift. As time passed and the afternoon came upon us, I continued my requests and without fail, the clouds obeyed me. It was then that I truly realized the power of thought and how much we actually can control in our lives if we maintain the connection to the divine oneness that exists without and within, just beneath the surface of our conditioned minds.

It was my last day, and although I had done vision quests alone up on the mountain, experienced sacred ceremonies and numerous sweat lodges, my ancestors had not yet come out to play. I asked Niyan to give me a bone reading using different bones, shells and other various parts of nature that he had accumulated over time. As he threw them and started reading their meanings from the way they fell, his faced changed. No longer was the Woodstock hippy sitting before me. It was an old Peruvian man, a man that was so deeply rooted in his culture that he lived and breathed it everyday. So much so that although he was born in another country, steeped in its own spirituality, he had traveled to remember who he was, to connect to his spiritual lineage, and had brought it back to share with the country he now called home.

As I watched how easily it came to him, it occurred to me that like many of us, he had not been trained explicitly, especially when the Calling first came. This knowledge that he had, came from somewhere else. A knowing from a past life? Or maybe just a connection to the universal oneness. Unlike me, he didn't have an identity issue. He wasn't searching for anything. His identity came from within. It didn't matter what the outside world thought or what genetics lay within the strands of his DNA. He knew who he was and lived it.

Before I took this journey, I was expecting someone to give me an answer to who I was. I was half expecting an ancestor to appear before my eyes and give me myself, to somehow give me a sense of belonging to one particular group or at least a humanistic generalization of a certain culture that I could pertain to, so I could say THIS IS ME and tick all the boxes associated with the expectation of what it is to belong to the African culture. I thought a Sangoma would be able to impart all this knowledge that I soon realized was always within me. Niyan was never meant to tell me anything but to just be there as a catalyst for my own self-realization. We were a lot alike, except he had chosen to listen to his calling, to listen to his spirit and the earth's, and live in accordance with what he heard. I decided that I was from that moment to be more like Ni Nixiwaka.

It's been over a year now since my experience in Sangoma Valley and I look back on that time and think how much I have grown. My ancestors did make an appearance when I least expected it. I realized that they were always there, imparting their knowledge through my unconscious mind. The thoughts that I had about belonging were just conditioned by my ego as a further way of separating me from my true divine nature, which always belongs to the oneness that is who we really are.

In truth, it doesn't matter what your DNA heritage is, or where you spent your past lives. Through the connection of being, you can access whatever feels right for you. With positive intentions of growth, you can evolve in whatever way you choose and always maintain your identity. By connecting to the earth and listening to the silent whispers she imparts, you can evolve. I give thanks for my experience because without going back to South Africa I would not have known that I didn't have to go there to be South African.

Reconnecting

I am the peace I seek.

Our deepest wounds come from feelings of separateness from Spirit. Yet Earth Mother's whispers are there to help us, even in the face of overwhelming self-doubt, to reconnect with Spirit. As each individual soul collaborates with Earth Mother, becoming healed and whole, many others benefit.

Or that I didn't have to give up one sense of identity for another; that my identity spans the ages and goes beyond labels of nationality.

Today when people ask me what my nationality is, I say 'Universal.' That fits me just fine.

How to Connect to Your Universal Oneness. Anywhere.

The most important thing about connecting to your true self is to silence the ego. Your Ego is all those thoughts in your mind that tell you that you can't do it or that you need something outside of yourself to be whole.

Many of these thoughts come from conditioning, and your past experience that has been shaped by societal influences throughout your trajectory of life so far. Sometimes other people are influential in those thoughts because they are the ones who have shaped your ideals about your identity. It is important to disconnect from those thoughts so that you can clear your conditioned beliefs about who you are.

A practical way of disconnecting is to cut the cords of conditioning. Think of a limiting belief that you have about yourself. Where did that idea come from? Did you hear it as a child as you grew up? Who was the person that first introduced you to that idea? And if it was yourself, who reinforced it?

Find a quiet area and close your eyes; take several deep breaths.
With each breath, the light fills your body. You can see the light being drawn into your nostrils with every inhale; imagine it being a silver and gold light. Allow yourself to feel the light moving through your body. It flows through to your lungs and transfers

to your blood stream. Soon your whole body is illuminated with the light. As this light begins to seep into your body; it gets brighter and brighter.

Scan the outside of your body. There will be holes in the light where you see cords attached. They may be thick like a tree trunk, or small and thin. Take your awareness or consciousness to one of the cords and feel who is attached to the other end. Ask what limiting belief or conditioning this cord delivers to you on a daily basis. Call upon Archangel Michael. Ask him to use his sword of truth and gently cut the cords and remove the egotistic idea. You may feel lighter and a sense of clarity may overcome you. Thank Archangel Michael. You can proceed to do this with all your cords if you wish.

To connect to the universal oneness, the best way is to silence your mind and open your heart chakra.

Go into a quiet place in nature. Close your eyes. Bring your awareness to the middle of your heart. Within the center of your heart lies an air-filled pouch that contains a burning white flame. Bring your awareness to the flame; breathe in and out and watch the flame slowly expand. Soon, it starts to change color. The colors change and flow until the first color repeats itself again. Notice how the color expands, slowly within you. Feel the peace within your heart. As the color bursts out into your auric field, it moves to envelop your etheric body, emotional body, your mental body and spiritual until it starts to merge with your surroundings, your city, the country and eventually the earth. Soon you and the stars, the planets, the universe are one. Sit in this oneness and feel the stillness and quiet tranquility of All That Is.

Open your eyes. Notice everything around you. Take a good look at the leaves on the trees, the blades of grass. Look at the sky, the clouds and the formations they make. Feel the ground beneath you and listen intently to the sounds around you. Once a sense of awe overwhelms you, you have connected to the universal oneness. Awe will turn to love and in turn, love will turn to peace.

When you are ready, close your eyes again. Feel the peace as your state of being. Know that this peace is just beneath the surface of your consciousness and can be accessed at any time through the flame within your heart. Watch the color retract through the universe, back through the stars, earth, your surroundings and your body and heart. Notice the flame return to its original size and again become white. Imagine tree roots sprouting from your feet and connecting to the earth.

By connecting to the divine universal oneness, you have the ability to access and be in flow with everything around you. This can open up possibilities that you never knew existed. By practicing the above exercise whenever you feel chaotic and disconnected, you can ensure that you are always connected to the divine.

Soon, peace will become your being.

Innocence

I am protected in all ways.

*There is a natural kindness and deep
wisdom in the pure heart of a child.
By freeing our imagination, allowing
ourselves to play, we become like
a child. Through reclaiming our
innocent nature, we realign ourselves
with the true essence of Spirit.*

CLARISSA HARISON

Lancaster, NY, USA

INSPIRED BY HER experiences with animals and nature, Clarissa Harison follows an intuitive-based approach toward holistic living. She combines her innate sensibilities of subtle environmental energies with ancient healing arts to initiate harmony, balance and empowerment for others. Her focus is on developing awareness of our relationship to the earth and inherent responsibility of stewardship of this planet.

Clarissa's BA in International Studies and interest in travel and languages led to working for a foreign embassy and various international corporations. Her innate design skills developed into working with individual clients to create beautiful, healthy environments. Clarissa has been trained in the ancient art of energetic harmonization of houses, buildings and environments and has studied with various internationally recognized masters. Among her various certifications are Interior Alignment®, Feng Shui and *The Complete Creative Process for Creating Gardens, Homes & Workplaces for the Soul.*

Currently residing in western New York, Clarissa is a writer, design professional and environmental intuitive who consults with businesses and individuals on how to improve their health and well being via their indoor and outdoor landscapes. An herbalist, organic gardener and licensed wildlife rehabilitator, Clarissa's repertoire includes knowledge of homeopathy, reiki, flower and mineral therapies, and shamanic techniques.

Clarissa's first article was published in 1994 describing a traumatic experience with a white-tailed deer, followed by subsequent environmental commentaries in local newspapers throughout the years. Her passion for nature and wildlife continues to inspire her and can be viewed at her blog www.awenenvironments.com.

Lady Muskoka:
A Story of Healing and Renewal

CLARISSA HARISON

Two years after my father's death my family returned to Lake Muskoka
with hopes of recapturing the joy we had experienced there in summers past.

*A*midst huge pink granite outcroppings around a freshwater lake formed by ancient Canadian glaciers, our week at Gravenhurst, Lake Muskoka, began with the powerful new moon solar eclipse and the intense astrological energies of the grand cross of July 2010 where four planets were squared, one in each of the elements of earth, air, fire and water.

I have traveled and lived in many places throughout my lifetime, but there are some that stay in your heart. Your relationship with them evolves over time. As I recall the events that took place during our last summer vacation at Lake Muskoka, I am filled with emotion. But the tears that form are not of sadness. They fall out of love and admiration for the beauty of this planet and the incredible inspiration and serenity that nature provides, when we choose to pay attention.

My story is one of healing and renewal for three generations, and it begins with my parents' *accidental* arrival at a cottage at Whitehead Farm on Lake Muskoka, Ontario, during the summer of 1954 where my brother would celebrate his second birthday. No reservations had been made. My father drove the four hours north from Buffalo, New York, across the Canadian border and into the province of Ontario on a tip from a co-worker. His motivation was great fishing and a vacation for his family. Though I would physically arrive in Gravenhurst seven years later, my first experience in this mystical region came while I was still in my mother's womb, as Mrs. Whitehead read my mother's tea leaves, telling her she would have a baby girl later that summer.

My fondest memories are of those family summers on Lake Muskoka: swimming, water skiing, fishing, making campfires and playing 'Indian' in the woods. Those were also my closest times with my father.

My parents were immigrants to the United States after World War II; my father was Russian and my mother German. Both grew up with tragedies created by war and politics. My father's father had been an aircraft engineer with strong political beliefs, hoping to undermine the policies of Stalin. He was eventually arrested and executed as a threat to the regime, as were millions of other Russians during that period. My grandmother was placed in a forced labor camp near Alma Alta, which is now Kazakhstan. She survived for over 20 years, only to die alone of a broken heart shortly after her release. Her husband was dead and her son had long since fled the country.

My father was orphaned at 14 and learned how to survive; escaping Russia and eventually meeting my mother years later in Germany, where he had been working. My parents later immigrated to the USA due to my father's constant fear of being sent back to Russia. And so they began their new life, though my father's memories would continue to haunt him wherever he went.

My mother's memories would follow her as well. Her five brothers died during World War II. Three perished on the Russian front and her 14 year old twin brothers were killed in March, 1945, just months before the war would officially end. They died in a bombing raid while apprenticed as carpenters. My grandfather identified the twins by their shoes. My mother had been living in the town of Stadtlohn, in the northern Rhine region of Germany, where over 86% of the town was destroyed during massive air strikes that year. Six hundred lives were lost including those of my two uncles.

My father never trusted anyone enough to discuss his early years, and took his secrets with him when he passed over in the fall of 2008. As a young girl, I understood nothing of my parents' pain; however, I now know that those summers spent at Lake Muskoka were healing for us all. It was the connection to the earth, to the water and to nature that brought us all together. These were truly happy times spent with my father. He taught me how to fish and water ski on that lake. It was not until much later in life that I began to understand how much my parents' pain and fear had been passed on to me, and my siblings.

Two years after my father's death, my family returned to Lake Muskoka with hopes of recapturing the joy and beauty we had experienced there in summers past. It was my brother who found a cottage on the very same bay where we had once camped. Little did we know as we headed off that summer towards an unfamiliar cottage, that we would have a very unique experience.

Ancestral Healing

Through love, I am the master of my own destiny.

Help arrives from the Spirit of Nature, where infinite possibilities lie, ensuring that our harmonious co-creations benefit others and balance events across time. In accordance with the Laws of Nature, our Higher Self sees beyond lifetimes of ancestral design, affirming our true soul destiny.

The morning of our trip did not begin on a positive note. Amidst packing and preparing to leave, I discovered that a side door would not lock. It was Saturday and I could not find a reliable locksmith on short notice. Knowing I would not feel at peace leaving all of my possessions and animals at risk, a wide range of disturbing emotions washed over me.

I began to question whether I should go at all. Financially it was a difficult time and I also felt uncomfortable leaving our pets in the care of someone else. Our recent move, as well as the stress and trauma of previous months, had left me physically and emotionally exhausted. Everything had been happening so fast that I could barely think clearly anymore.

I really needed this vacation to rejuvenate myself, but I also questioned whether the lock not closing was a message telling me not to leave – that something awful might happen during our trip. I had made a firm commitment to my family and I truly didn't want to disappoint anyone by not going. I decided to allow my 8 year old son to go ahead without me in the company of my brother, while our neighbor managed to temporarily fix the door so that it could at least be secured.

Instinctively, I began to feel that something would occur at Lake Muskoka this year that would make all this effort and frustration worthwhile. I called my mother and we set off on our four hour trip. I can't say that the rest of the day went any better. We had a long wait at the border, and, irritable that my brother had not waited for us, I took a wrong turn and headed in another direction. My brother had a similar frustrating experience. By the time we all arrived, we had been on the road for 5 ½ hours and everyone was in a foul mood except for my son. Max was thrilled to once again be in Gravenhurst!

Lake Muskoka is approximately 200 km north of the large city of Toronto, Ontario. Gravenhurst is located in the southeast corner of this lake region and is considered the gateway to Muskoka due to its unique and varied heritage. It was also the home of Canada's first sanatorium, built in 1897. Unfortunately, this center is now empty and in disrepair, but the sacredness of the land and the healing white pines and cedars remain.

The cedars, which are everywhere, are sacred to many Native American tribes including the Cherokee, who believe them to contain the spirit of their ancestors. Interestingly, the Siberian cedar is also a sacred tree to the Russians and believed to hold the energy of the cosmos, offering many healing gifts to those who honor them. No wonder my father loved spending time amongst these trees.

The Muskoka Lake region was originally inhabited by Native Americans of the Algonquin, Ojibwa (also known as Chippewa) and Huron tribes. Some say the name Muskoka originated from the Chippewa Chief, Mesqua Ukee, whose name means 'not easily turned back in the day of battle.' Others say it came from the Huron, meaning 'the place where the large rocks are red.'

The Europeans initially ignored this region, home to the Ojibwa tribe who used it for fishing, hunting and trapping. Though thousands of settlers were given 200 acres of free land around 1865, many gave up or turned to road building, lumbering or tourism because the land was covered with ubiquitous rocks, making it unsuitable for farming. The pink granite rocks in this region exude a powerful vibration. According to geologists, this granite is some of the oldest on earth.

Not knowing what to expect from the cottage we had chosen, I was pleasantly surprised to experience an immediate sense of the sacred on this property. Rest areas had been strategically placed throughout the groves of cedars, taking advantage of the positioning of the sun throughout the day, creating unique sites for contemplation.

A huge boulder rested on the beachfront, on top of which was a display of carefully positioned rocks called an *inukshuk* – the Inuit word describing the piles of rock slabs and stone found throughout the Canadian Arctic, often built to resemble a person with arms outstretched. While these rock displays were sometimes used as markers for passageways or food storage, they also functioned as spiritual sites, either built in memory of a loved one or to mark a place of respect. This structure immediately conveyed a strong feeling of sacredness to me.

I have great admiration for the way these stone markers are created, and the powerful spiritual message they have come to represent. They are no longer just stone markers; they are a symbol of cooperation, leadership and the human spirit. Although each stone is a separate entity, it has specifically been chosen for how well it fits together with the other stones. Each stone supports the one above and is supported by another below, securing the structure through balance. The stones achieve unity and strength by working together. How appropriately this structure represents the interdependence of life on this planet. Rather than thinking solely of our own individual needs, we can achieve greater success by relying on friendship, support and cooperation with one another, as well as with this planet.

We discovered shells and brightly colored blue glass stones carefully strewn about in the water around the inukshuk, left there by the owners. Max was delighted to find one treasure after another in the beach waters. The next day, I set out to create a tiny altar of crystals and other special objects around the inukshuk, to enhance the sacredness I already felt, and to link my objects with the energy found there. In the center, I placed a small candle which I lit later that evening to activate the energies of this outdoor altar to nature. Meanwhile, I spent my day swimming and connecting with the essence of the lake – the goddess or divine spirit of the waters of Muskoka.

Throughout the ages, ancient civilizations have worshipped water as the source of all life. Its rejuvenating qualities are widely known. That day I began to remember how much I loved swimming and the freedom it allowed me. I delighted in just floating in the water, relieving the stress of the journey and the last few months, allowing my thoughts to drift into meditation. All my cares began to transform and release as I immersed myself in the peace and serenity of these waters, becoming one with Lady Muskoka.

Imagine my surprise when I found a huge raw crystal of milky and smoky quartz embedded along the shoreline. In that moment I knew I was meant to arrive at this destination and experience the sacredness of this land and these waters once again. This crystal would always remind me of my days spent here, and all the gifts we eventually would receive from the waters and shores of Muskoka.

The following day was my brother's birthday. He had risen early and surprised us with a huge pike caught earlier that morning. It had been years since my brother caught a fish of that caliber. His intention had been only to show us the pike and release him, but it soon became apparent that the pike was losing its life force. We were all saddened and equally surprised because pike are considered the 'water wolf' of fresh lakes, with very aggressive behavior and voracious appetites. I made a last attempt to help revive this beautiful fish by swimming with him in the deeper, cool waters of the lake.

Unfortunately, the pike would swim a short way on his own, only to turn on his side once again. It was with great regret that we all recognized this fish would not recover. It seemed an unnecessary death for us all. I lay him on the boulder alongside the inukshuk to honor the life he had given for our dinner that evening. This fish had apparently made a choice on this special day.

As a result of my close relationship with the natural world, I often receive internal guidance which I know is the spirit of the land speaking to me. Being here was no exception. This time I was inspired to build an outdoor mandala to further anchor the sacredness that I was feeling on this land and to offer my own contribution to nature.

I gathered my new large crystal, all the shells and cobalt blue stones that Max had collected, together with my other crystals, and created a beautiful mandala activated by a candle in the center. I also placed drops of essences made from the vibrations of gemstones and orchids from sacred sites in the Andes, linking these two lands. I said some prayers to the earth, to this place, and gave thanks for being guided here. Despite the many challenges at the outset of this trip, I had found a renewed sense of peace.

Later that same day, my brother returned excited from a boat trip, saying he had found an incredible island of birds out on the lake. In all the years of coming to this area, we had never known of such a place. There were blue herons, loons, seagulls, turkey vultures and a multitude of other birds I could not identify. It was an island wildlife sanctuary, filled with trees and nests, where no man was allowed to set foot.

The mystical theme continued as the week progressed. I would swim three times a day, exercising, as well as soothing my body, connecting with the essence of the water and creating a special water meditation each day. Being familiar with the work of Dr. Emoto, a Japanese researcher who discovered the amazing effect our thoughts and prayers can have on an entire body of water, my intention was to bless and instill my love for these waters of Muskoka and communicate its sacredness.

In essence, I hoped my actions would also help mitigate the harmful affects of the BP oil spill that had occurred in the Gulf of Mexico earlier that year. Despite being geographically distant, these waters were still linked energetically via the very nature of water. By offering prayer and my intentions for healing, this could in effect support healing for both bodies of water. Each day I repeated my prayers and focused my intentions on healing the waters of Muskoka and the Gulf area, as well as all the waters of the earth, those within us and part of All That Is.

The morning following the discovery of the bird sanctuary, I began my early swim amidst a peaceful meditation, simply floating as before. I was so engrossed in the buoyancy, love and peacefulness I was feeling, that I did not notice a loon that had been swimming alongside me the entire time. Anyone who is familiar with these birds knows of their haunting voice and mystical qualities. Because of my inner peace and joy, the bird was not intimidated nor threatened by my presence and continued to dive for fish only a few feet away. Eventually the loon's diving escapades drew it further away from me, but I will never forget that moment of complete heart/spirit connection with this beautiful, graceful bird. I later learned that Native American tribes view this bird as a divine messenger associated with peace and harmony.

Our next visitors that day were a flock of Canadian geese, a wild turkey with her baby meandering through the woods, a squadron of ducks, two separate flocks of loons, two baby otters frolicking alongside the shoreline, and lastly, a blue heron fishing along the beachfront. It had been an amazing wildlife-filled experience! Later that evening, I realized that it would have been my Dad's 87th birthday.

We would continue to have more wildlife visitations the following day, ending with the grand finale of a brown bear rummaging around near the cottage in search of food. I remembered my Dad always joking about being strong "like a Russian bear." I welled up inside as the date and significance of all these visitors touched my heart.

I cannot help but think these animals, which continued to be magically drawn to this property, were somehow my Dad's way of saying he was okay and watching over us, and happy that we were there. Gravenhurst had been a place where he had healed some of the painful memories of the past. It became a place of healing for all of us – three generations in fact. As the days continued, I saw other signs – a circle of cedar trees on one peninsula, a symbol of sacredness to the Druids and other ancient cultures. And wildlife continued to appear wherever we went.

The venerable beauty of the Lake Muskoka region cannot be denied. Its landscape has such a healing, spiritual quality, bringing peace and serenity to all who seek it. Despite the prolific development that has taken place since my childhood visits, with many old cottages being torn down and grander ones built everywhere, this land remains powerful, sacred and unique.

There were other incidences both big and small which made this vacation an unusual and deeply spiritual experience for me. Without having met or spoken to the proprietors, it was obvious they cared deeply about this property and had created an intimate atmosphere by making use of the naturally occurring energies of this land. Following the rhythm of the sun to site rest places is a very ancient way of living in alignment with the land and nature. The endearing touch of magical treasures strewn about the beach waters would also captivate the joy and imagination of any child. These owners had truly created a spiritual, healing and rejuvenating experience for everyone who found rest at their cottage.

It is a magical combination when humans take the time to accentuate and enhance the already powerful earth energies that are present in a location. Not only did this setting draw the spirits of a variety of different animals, but it also led us to other places previously unknown to my family throughout the many years of vacationing in this area.

My one last gift from Lady Muskoka came from these owners – a beautiful photograph of the full moon rising in the evening sky, the inukshuk and the beach-front that I had admired on so many occasions. Taken by a guest one summer, this photo continues to inspire me with the serenity and healing magic of Muskoka.

Mandala for Healing the Past
I believe that memories are passed on through generations in a variety of ways, though the descendents have never actually experienced those events. These memories live on through the etheric body (human energy field) and via our DNA, held tightly within our cells until they are released through some form of energetic healing or manipulation of our genes. New research in Scandinavia involving epigenetics has shown that the DNA of descendants of families who have experienced famine and starvation during many previous generations is adversely affected, leaving "an imprint on genetic material in eggs and sperm."[1] Descendents were shown to suffer from a variety of health problems associated with this experience of lack. We are now seeing the emergence of a blend of science and spirituality, as this knowledge was previously unknown to modern day scientists. Dr. Alberto Villoldo, a Cuban born anthropologist and shaman, has written of his own experiences with energetic imprints passed on from his father's memories of trauma and lack. Through this combined research, we find that memories or traumas can also be transmitted via thoughts, words, mannerisms, actions and choices that generations make on a continual basis.

Unless resolved, any negative imprints could potentially interfere with a descendant's aspirations and foundations for a healthy, joyful and balanced life. By recognizing and understanding this ancestral trauma and pain, as well as the patterns which result and perpetuate, we can begin to resolve them. By doing so, we change our destinies, as well as those of future generations.

It is believed that we can also go back in time. Quantum physics has demonstrated that the time continuum we have created does not in fact exist. It is merely a device that we as humans have created to monitor our experiences.

Within the shamanic world, a place that transcends the human boundaries of fear and limitation, what we heal within ourselves moves backward in time to heal our family and ancestors. Despite the fact that my father never spoke much of his past nor was he very communicative throughout his lifetime, I know that my return to Lake Muskoka was a source of healing for *all* of us.

I don't think that our travels are random. I know that we all end up exactly where we are supposed to be in order to heal those aspects of ourselves that will enable us to complete our soul's journey toward wholeness. You can travel to well-known sacred sites, or you can find peace and renewal within a home where the inhabitants have made a conscious effort to create their own sacred space.

Creating an altar, or mandala, to your ancestors is one such way to begin healing the past. By gathering objects representing your ancestors and the four elements of earth, air, fire and water, you can create a powerful source of transformation to initiate your healing journey.

To create your own source of healing, begin by placing together in a circle or spiral, items such as:

- photos of your family, grandparents and other ancestors
- crystals, rocks and other objects from nature
- special objects such as jewelry, mementos and other treasured items
- writings and artwork created by ancestors
- fresh flowers, spring water or a child's photo to represent new life
- flower, mineral and environmental essences from sacred places to provide healing vibrations

This circular pattern represents the continuity of life, of death and rebirth, and how the lessons that we experience come back around in order to heal us. Carl Jung viewed the mandala as a representation of the unconscious self, a tool leading to wholeness. By recognizing the imprints we carry and placing their representations together, you are acknowledging that your ancestors and your experiences have all contributed to the unique individual that you are now.

A candle placed in the center activates the spirit of your ancestors and also brings the past to completion through the symbolic death and rebirth created by fire. Prayers said over your mandala will carry via your breath, the element of air, and be transformed by the fire of your candle to bring renewal and peace. The more prayers and intentions directed at your altar, the more healing and transformative it will be. An altar placed outdoors can be even more powerful, especially when located over strong earth energies.

The most potent source of healing energy is made available when nature collaborates with man. Nature can be so generous and inspirational when we open ourselves up to its amazing wisdom and bountiful beauty. What previously seemed unimaginable, such as swimming with a loon on a beautiful morning – this merging into oneness – falls into the realm of possibility. There is no limit to this collaboration and the awesome gifts it can produce.

It is our connection to this earth which supports our physical being, while nurturing and healing our soul. When we honor the rhythms of the earth and the sacredness of all life, we inherently heal those aspects of ourselves which we believe to be unworthy or imperfect, to move beyond our own self-perceived failings and limitations. We find that place of peace, of silence and sacredness, where all things are possible and the magnificence of our being is reflected in the beauty around us.

Only when we understand the past we have inherited and follow our own inner guidance, can we begin to create a new outcome for ourselves and our future descendents. That is, after all, the vision for the new paradigm here on earth.

❧

1 Cloud, John, *Why Your DNA Isn't Your Destiny*, Time Magazine, January 6, 2010.

Bibliography
Emoto, Masaru, *The True Power of Water*, Beyond Words Publishing, Inc., 2005.
Jung, C.G., Aniela Jaffé, *Memories, Dreams, Reflections*, Random House, 1965.
Megré, Vladimir, *Anastasia*, Ringing Cedars Press, 1996.
Villoldo, Alberto, *Shaman, Healer, Sage*, Crown Publishing Group, December 2000.

JUDY WARD
Kingston, Ontario, Canada

JUDY WARD HAS been pursuing her own journey of spiritual growth and emotional healing for many years. She currently teaches many different forms of holistic healing, spiritual growth, and energy work at local community colleges and independently through her holistic teaching and treatment practice called "Search for Spirit." Judy has trained with many of the world's recognized leaders in holistic, spiritual, physical and emotional health and brings this knowledge and learning to her practice. She has a passion for sharing and teaching and always treats her clients and students with compassion and understanding.

Judy is certified in Usui Reiki, Karuna Reiki, Integrated Energy Therapy and is an Angel Therapy Practitioner®, Certified by Doreen Virtue. She is a Certified Counselling Hypnotist and Past Life Regressionist and Life Between Lives Regressionist, as well as a professional Soul Coach, Certified by Denise Linn. To honor her teaching journey, Judy studied two years to become a Certified Teacher of Adults. Judy is a lifelong learner who is passionate about teaching, hiking, animals and reading uplifting books.

Judy now lives in a small village just outside of Kingston, Ontario, Canada called Battersea. For consultations, Soul Coaching sessions, readings, treatments or workshops, contact Judy at judy.ward@sympatico.ca or check out her website at www.searchforspirit.ca

A Deeper Perspective

JUDY WARD

❧

Today was the day we would tour the ruins of
an ancient Incan city – Machu Picchu.

It was 4:30 in the morning, as our group of ten huddled in front of our hotel on a deserted street in a foreign country. It was dark; we were tired and yet the air was electric. You could feel the excitement in the air. This is what we had come for!

Simon, our guide, had promised us that if we caught the 4:30 a.m. bus, we would be the first to arrive and enter the gates to our destination in Peru, securing the most desirable view point. Our mission was to experience this magical, spiritual place at sunrise. With anticipation, I awaited the high point of our trip. Today was the day we would tour the ruins of an ancient Incan city – Machu Picchu.

Being a spiritual person has led me to many ancient sites. I had already experienced the Pyramids, the Sphinx and the Temple of Isis in Egypt, as well as Chichen Itza in Mexico. Each of these sites has a story to tell and its own energy to feel. Today would be the most spectacular. Even as my expectations were soaring, I tried to keep them under control, knowing full well that expectations can lead to disappointment.

As we quietly waited for our transportation, out of the darkness meandered a small Peruvian woman carrying trays of sandwiches and coffee. Wherever I travel, I am always amazed to see the ingenious ways the locals invent to make an income from the so predictable tourists.

Suddenly our bus careened around the corner. After a short boarding process, we were on our way. The ride to our destination would take approximately 30 minutes. As the bus crawled up the mountain through many switchbacks, my mind wandered back to the beginning of our trip when we had first met our guide. Simon had described the magnificence of this ancient place and what a spectacular sight it was to behold, as the first rays of sunlight danced across the city of stone, leaving sparkling designs and patterns. We were spurred by his description not to miss this breathtaking experience. Here at last, was the day it was to happen!

Simon was a unique tour leader who took the time to discover the needs of each person in his group and provided individual experiences for each of us. Having discovered that I am a spiritual person, he had arranged for a few of us (but mainly for me) to participate in a private tour, plus a ceremony with a local Shaman, following our usual tourist tour. Only four of us would attend this ceremony which would take place in a private, sheltered alcove in the midst of Machu Picchu. I awaited this experience with eager anticipation.

As the bus pulled into the parking area just ahead of the gates, once again the excitement began to rise. As promised, we were the first people to enter the gates as they opened. With Simon in the lead, we raced up the mountain path through the darkness. It was an incredibly steep trail, and my lungs ached as I ran – higher and higher. The altitude and exertion were agonizing, yet our excitement overrode any pain as we continued to race towards our destination – which, according to Simon, was the best place to view the sunrise. And suddenly, there it was: the Watchman's cabin, or the ruins of it. No one else had arrived ahead of us at this prime location for the perfect view.

It was still dark as we found our places atop the ledge of this coveted spot above the city of stone. Slowly others began to arrive, all of us excitedly awaiting the breaking of dawn. But to my dismay, the clouds moved in. I prayed they would clear, but it was not to be. We would not get to see the sun's rays dancing over the stones in gorgeous shimmering patterns. I could feel disappointment creeping in. I pushed aside those feelings and decided to carry on and enjoy what was. After all, here we were in Peru at an ancient Incan city and it would still be a spectacular sight to behold from our perch high above the ruins.

As dawn broke and light filled the sky, it was easy to see that this was a massive city sitting on the top of a mountain, itself surrounded by towering green mountains bathed in light. This was worth it and I allowed my disappointment to dissipate. Long ago I learned to keep going and make the best of what is, even if it is not exactly as I had imagined. And, once again, I learned the lesson that high expectation is bound to cause disappointment. It is best to just stay open to whatever will appear. Often this alone can bring amazing surprises.

As daylight arrived, it was time for us to make the trek back down the mountain and meet up with our local tour guide for a history lesson on Machu Picchu. As we began our descent, we noticed llamas standing on top of the mountain soaking up the sun. Had they arrived after us or were they always there and yet unseen by us due to the darkness? It was now apparent that hundreds of tourists were there as well.

After our descent, we were met by a local guide who proceeded to give us the history of this amazing place as we wandered from site to site, room to room and building to building. It was fascinating to learn that this city was built at the top of this mountain by the Incas and that the conquering Spaniards never found it. I could readily understand why, after that bus trip and the race up the mountain. I pictured the Incans making that trip without the assistance of those roads and paths. Yes, brilliant they were, for no one would have believed that this massive city could have been constructed here.

It was discovered by an American, Hiram Bingham in 1911. As the site was excavated, it was found to be quite well preserved. Some people believe that this was a defensive location, but the ruins suggested to some archaeologists that Machu Picchu was more of a religious center. Excavations revealed that many of the people who lived here were women, and because numerous objects found here were religious artifacts, it was thought that these women were most likely Priestesses.

We saw the agricultural sector where people grew their food, the manufacturing sector, the Sun Temple, the Temple with three windows, buildings used for housing and the remains of a massive sun dial. It was all wonderfully historical but once again, I felt disappointment mounting. Where was the magic, or the energetic experience I had so longed for? It just didn't happen amongst the throngs of people, the heat, the noise and the chatter. It was interesting enough, but not what I had dreamed of experiencing. Being very sensitive to energy, I have often had mystical experiences in ancient ruins, but that didn't happen here. The tour lasted about an hour and upon completion, Simon delivered my husband Brian and I, and another couple to the local Shaman.

He was dressed in traditional Peruvian clothing, wearing a leather hat and carrying a bundle under his arm wrapped in a woven red Peruvian blanket. On the way to our quiet and private location amongst the ruins, he pointed out energy portals and crevices that led to underground cities. One site contained a stone altar with well worn hand prints in it. He suggested we place our hands in those positions and rest our forehead against the stone altar. We learned that this was how the Incans had activated their third eye.

On the night of the full moon, the moon's rays shone on exactly that spot, energizing the stone altar. I could feel energy everywhere and it was amazing. He conveyed to us how the sun and moon's rays played an important role in where people chose to sit, and why some windows in the three-windowed temple were closed in and others left open – this was for the sun and the moon's rays. He showed us where the priestesses sat so that the moon's rays could shine on them. In the previous tour, these had just been stone stools in the pathway. It amazed me how different two tours of exactly the same site could be.

Suddenly I had an important realization. The first tour satisfied the logical, left side of the brain, while this tour satisfied the more creative, intuitive side of the brain. Together they created magic. It reminded me that we need to use and balance both sides of our brain to experience magic and yet stay grounded in the real world.

As we meandered amongst the ruins towards our ceremony destination, the Incan culture came alive for me through the Shaman's words and visions. I sensed the truth of what he was describing deep in my inner being as I felt the energy of these sacred spots. This was what I had longed to experience. I felt as if I was a part of this ancient culture.

Upon arrival at our private location amongst the ruins, he spread out the red patterned blanket on the ground and lovingly placed each of his ceremonial articles on the blanket. They included a conch shell, a rattle, a dish with herbs that I imagined to be sage and a large turkey feather. There was also a local plant (coca leaves) that he proceeded to chew.

We sat in a semi circle around him. He asked each of us to set an inner intention for the ceremony. Many passing people peered in to this quiet alcove, but no one dared to enter. It was as if he had put up an energy shield that said 'Do Not Enter.' As they peered in, they seemed to sense that something sacred was happening and never dared to cross the threshold. The Shaman blew on the conch shell to call in the spirits, lit the herbs, fanning them with the feather, and then began to rattle. All the while, he chanted unintelligible words in his native Quechuan language.

From this location, he pointed out a portal across the mountain that was directly in line with where we sat. As I looked towards this area, I could feel the energy and the truth of this portal in every cell of my body. Throughout the ceremony, my eyes were again and again drawn to that portal – it seemed as though I were a moth drawn to the flame, so strong was the energy. The ceremony itself lasted about 20 minutes and felt extremely sacred – an amazing experience!

Later I compared the differences between these two tours of exactly the same place. They were two entirely different perspectives. As I mulled this over, the two melded together into my being and a realization dawned in my heart and mind. It was having experienced both sides and both perspectives that made this experience so special and so sacred to me. We need the more physical experience to keep us grounded in the real world, but it is the spiritual experience that brings magic and imagination into play. Together they can make life so much more exciting.

Pondering this realization, I knew that our life experiences are just like this. There are always different perspectives to every experience. It was a profound learning and I knew it to be absolute truth. I began looking for the different meanings or experiences elsewhere, and this has had a profound effect on my life. I noticed that by changing my attitude or my perception, everything changed with it.

Just like at Machu Picchu, where I had experienced two completely different perspectives, so too can this be applied to ordinary life. Many of the experiences we have in our everyday physical existence seem one dimensional, but each one of them also contains a more spiritual experience, just waiting to be discovered. Now when I am struggling with an experience or feeling disappointed in any way, I look for a different or deeper perspective.

One of my recent life experiences demonstrates this principle very well. If you have cared for your elderly parents, struggling with their care while trying to live your own life, you may find this familiar. Perhaps my experience can open new possibilities and a new perspective for you.

About six years ago I had taken on the job of caring for my aging ex-father-in-law, Josef. He didn't drive and was unable to get to town for groceries, banking and other necessities. For a few years I simply picked him up once a week and drove him into town for banking, groceries, shopping and we always went to Tim Horton's for coffee and a blueberry fritter. Then I drove him home, helped him pay his bills and left again to resume my normal life. The whole process took about 3 or 4 hours and I simply built that time into my schedule. This weekly ritual made him so happy and he was always appreciative of the effort I made to be there for him.

As he continued to age, his health began to deteriorate and his care became more of a challenge. Even with the assistance of daily morning Home Care, I spent an enormous amount of time cooking, cleaning, shopping, paying bills and caring for this poor 94 year old soul who was so alone. He began to depend on me more and more and his care began to consume more of my time and my life. I found myself running to his home almost every day and sometimes spending the day at the hospital with him when he fell and injured himself. Every day, he required more and more care.

As his condition continued to deteriorate and his needs increased, it became too much for me to handle on my own. I hired some help. That did alleviate some of the pressure, but even with this assistance and daily Home Care, he still required a tremendous amount of my time and energy. He also became more difficult to deal with as his paranoia grew. He started hiding his food so no one would steal it, and to hide the fact that he was becoming incontinent. I was exhausted and as my frustration and exhaustion grew, I found myself becoming angry and resentful of this drain on my time and energy. Where was the time for my husband and my own life? And yet, having a keen sense of responsibility, I carried on.

I seemed to be alone in this process as it continued to consume more and more of me. One day while complaining to my sister, she said, "Do you feel that you can walk away from this?" I responded "No, there is nobody else." Her reply was "Then, do it with love." Those words struck me deeply. I had been seeing this situation with Josef as a burden and a responsibility that was consuming me. I needed to shift my perspective and look deeper. As I searched for another perspective, I discovered that this situation was an opportunity for a major spiritual lesson for me that I had been missing.

I have been a holistic practitioner and spiritual teacher for 15 years. During that time, my goal with my students has always been to help them to shift and heal. I truly wanted to make a difference in their lives. This was the vision of my mission as a teacher and practitioner. As I shifted my perspective about Josef, I had a profound realization. If my goal was to make a difference in someone else's life, was I not making a difference in this one soul's life?

Another part of me was given the opportunity to learn an important spiritual lesson. If you want to make a difference in someone else's life, you must come from love. I began to shift my perspective from one of duty and responsibility to one of love and making a difference in this one person's life. It became very clear to me that through my actions I was in fact, fulfilling my mission. I had just not seen it that way before, because this is not how I had personally envisioned my mission.

Once I had this realization, it changed everything for me and made it easier for me to accept and perform these tasks from a loving perspective.

Shortly after that, as his care became more and more impossible for us to handle, Josef was admitted to a nursing home. I could have walked away at that point but with my new perspective, I continued to visit him at least once a week, shop for his needs and pay his bills. I took him for walks, bought and wrapped his family Christmas presents, and arranged family birthday and Christmas parties for him. When I was with him, I gave him my full attention. I did however put some boundaries around the amount of time I was giving. This I called loving myself and taking care of myself and my own family.

Josef often took his frustrations out on me, but again I was able to see that was exactly what he was doing. I didn't take it personally. And each time before I left, he always offered appreciative words, like "Good you came" and "I love you." The difference I was making in his life was visible. He passed away last year and I look back without regret for the time I spent and the lessons I learned. I know that I truly made a difference in the last years of his life. This for me has become a blessing and a gift.

Often we have a vision of what we think our purpose in life is or our mission. But when it doesn't happen the way we think it should, we are disappointed. However, when we look at things from a deeper perspective, we may find that we are doing exactly what we are supposed to be doing – just not in the way we had expected or anticipated. It is an important truth I'm glad I discovered. My time with Josef became a gift and a blessing not only to him as a support system and a care giver, but to me as well, by providing growth and learning on my own spiritual path.

Now in my teaching practice, I often see some of my students going through this same experience of looking after aging parents, and I am able to share with them what I learned. It helps them to shift their perspective and allows them to come from a different space – a space of love. Making this shift can make the daunting task of looking after our aging parents so much easier. Sharing my story has become my gift to them. Life's experiences, even when challenging, can be such a gift of learning.

Just like my experiences at Machu Picchu and with Josef, when things didn't go exactly as I had planned, my emotions took over and I let them negatively affect my experience. When I tried to control everything and make it go the way I wanted it to, life was a challenge. When I allowed a different perspective to arise, then the magic began. And this continues every time I follow this process.

It is not always easy to see the other perspective when we get caught up in the emotions and frustration of our challenges. If we ask our higher self, our Angels or our Creator for help in seeing another perspective, we are always given the answer. In my case, the answer came from my sister and her wise message. Long after Josef passed on, I thanked my sister for her wise words and told her how much she had helped me. She didn't even remember saying them. But for me they had been the answer to my prayers. The universe works in mysterious ways. It prompted me to remember that when we ask for help, we must be open to how the answer might come.

Often we try to control our experiences instead of letting guidance lead us. When we have a vision of how things should come to us, we often are not open to how the universe wants to bring it to us in a different way.

Another life experience demonstrated for me the value of being open to how things come for us. I had decided to make a vision board for the New Year ahead. A vision board is a collection of photos, words, colors and scenes that represent the goals and dreams we would like to manifest. We collect these representations from magazines, photos and other sources, and then paste them onto poster board. A vision board is a tool that we can use to visually focus on our goals. The Law of Attraction says that when we regularly give our goals positive attention, they will manifest much more quickly. By having our dreams in a visual format, it makes it easier to focus on them daily. Denise Linn, one of my teachers, says that when you create a vision board for your future, you bring the unseen into form and ground it into the physical world.

One of the photos I placed on the vision board I was creating was a pair of hands demonstrating auras. Above the photo I placed the words 'seeing auras.' My intention was to see auras with my third eye. I have since learned that when you are manifesting your dreams and goals, you must be very specific about what you want.

Shortly after creating this vision board, I began to think a lot about purchasing an aura and chakra photography camera. Though it was expensive, I jumped right in and ordered it. It just seemed right to me somehow. There were many struggles in getting it set up and working, but I persevered. Sometimes we have to prove we are willing to go the distance for something we really want.

With the camera now up and running, I am able to see my own and other people's auras and chakras. These photographs say a lot about what is going on in our lives and in which areas we need to work. I realized that this was an incredible manifestation of one of the goals from my vision board. Once again, I learned that we can put our goals and dreams out there, but they may not come exactly in the way we had intended. We must remain open and allow them to manifest as

Appreciation

I give thanks for the blessings I receive.

When we begin to see life's events with an open mind and clear vision, detached from emotion or judgment, we receive the gift of understanding. From this state of inner peace comes appreciation. Appreciation inspires spontaneous gratitude toward everything and everyone in our lives.

the universe wishes us to have them. The aura machine, which also photographs our chakras, showing their balances or imbalances, has become a blessing in my work as a holistic spiritual practitioner and teacher. It is a tool that I use to track my own progress and the progress of my students as they do their healing work.

So when you are feeling frustrated and challenged in your physical experiences, no matter where you are located, look for the spiritual lesson to bring magic into your life. Just like my experience while traveling to Machu Picchu, know that there is always a deeper perspective to every experience. By incorporating this information into my everyday life, I have found the gift of learning and growth for myself, in looking after an aging parent and in being open to how my dreams and goals manifest themselves into my life. And you can do it too.

Finding the Gift

Sit quietly by yourself with a journal and a pen, and write down an experience that is challenging you currently in your life. Write down all the details about it, including your feelings, your thoughts and any other sensations that you become aware of. Notice if this is a physical, mental or emotional challenge.

Next, sit quietly and ask your Higher Self, your Angels or your Creator, for guidance. Ask how you can see this situation in another way. Is there a deeper perspective that you are not seeing, or is there some lesson that you need to learn? Wait for the answer. If one does not come right away, try again tomorrow. Wait patiently for your answer. It will come. Stay open to what others are saying, conversations that you overhear and books that beckon you to them. Step out of your frustration and disappointment and be open to how your answer may come to you. Know that everything that happens, happens for a reason, and our most challenging situations usually hold the most profound lessons for us.

Once you receive your answer, try to incorporate these new ideas into your life. Change can often be frightening, so begin by making little changes in the way you think or perceive something. Feel love in your heart for the situation or the persons involved. Try to see their good qualities. Forgive those involved, and yourself if necessary. Journal all of your insights and the changes you make. Notice how your life begins to shift and change when you change your perception of the challenge to a learning experience or a spiritual truth. Find the gift in every situation.

Encouragement

I am guided by love and wisdom.

We trust that the right teacher arrives when needed, even if in disguise. Through the encouragement of Spirit and many mentors, our impact on the world grows. We share these blessings by generously encouraging all those whose lives we touch.

ROBERTA ASHKAWA BINDER
Western North Carolina

BORN AND RAISED in Eastern Pennsylvania, Roberta relocated to Colorado where she found a new world of research and exploration waiting. Native American Elders soon stepped into her life bringing opportunities for drum making, ritual, ceremony, and myths to explode into truth. Relocating once again to the mountains of Western North Carolina, Roberta lives in the homeland of the Cherokee. She realizes that, without question, each step she takes is on Sacred Ground and she quietly acknowledges the stories as the planet whispers its wisdom to all who listen.

Roberta has incorporated her Feng Shui, Geomancy and Space Clearing mastery into an active Feng Shui practice. Her studies have included masters and mentors from around the world. Additionally, both Oglala Lakota and Cherokee Elders have deepened her innate knowings of Earth Energies, Space Clearing, Energy Sensitivities and Sacred Space. She is a respected teacher and facilitates ceremony, seminars and retreats.

A writer and editor, Roberta has participated in numerous books, both as writer and editor. She is currently ghostwriting the memoirs of an internationally known musician and music agent through RobertaEdits.com. She is a regular contributor to *WNC Woman*, a regional publication serving Western NC and surrounding area.

With a lifelong researcher's passion for history and a deep love of all Earth Mother's beings, Roberta walks with the words of the Ogala Lakota: "Mitakuye Oyasin" – "We are ALL related."

Roberta invites you to explore her website SacredEarthWisdom.com.

Walking on the Sacred Land
of the Oglala Lakota

ROBERTA ASHKAWA BINDER

To the Lakota, the land belongs to no one; it is for all to care for and share.

This land, we call the United States, was believed by the Indians to belong to no one. It was to be shared with all Nations and Tribes… to be shared in Peace with all, until the Europeans arrived and thought the Indians were barbarians, to be pushed aside.

I was born and raised in Eastern Pennsylvania, once home of the Lenape Nation. Philadelphia, to be exact, known as the cradle of history for the United States, the seat of government for the newly formed United States of America where the drafting of the Declaration of Independence and the Constitution took place. The entire North Eastern seaboard had been involved in the battles to establish independence from England. And the indigenous people who lived in this country, those we called the Indians… they were nomads, easily removed to other lands, since the forefathers felt they *deserved* to own these new territories that these *natives* had called home.

As a child, the circle of friends I ran with had a favorite game of Cowboys and Indians. I always wanted to be an Indian; in fact, nothing less than being Chief kept me happy. Even into adulthood, I continue to maintain, "I'm not a very good Indian, but I'm a great Chief." I don't believe I fully realized the full meaning of those words. To be called Chief is a title to be earned through valor, through leadership skills; it is bestowed with great honor… and great responsibility.

Born in the sun sign of Taurus, I have always held a deep love of Earth Mother. My childhood was spent mostly in a country landscape, where I was free to run in the woods, hike the local mountains, explore streams, grow vegetables and fruit, climb trees and swim in local lakes. I loved to throw myself on the ground and watch the birds and clouds float by.

Cacoosing (owl), Catasauqua (thirsty earth), Neversink (at the promontory), Wyomissing (great meadows), Tulpehocken (turtle island)…

My neighborhood was sprinkled with areas that were known by their Indian name, be it small communities, streams, schools, street names and even counties. On the other hand, there was no indication that any indigenous peoples continued to live in the area. I never questioned where or why they had disappeared. I recognized that the Lenape had at one time been plentiful and had lived in the tri-state area peacefully for generations and yet, never once did I question why they were no longer present. I can only guess that I assumed they walked among us, *the invaders.*

Although we learned a smattering of indigenous peoples' studies in school, it was only a brief passing over in a very surface manner. And for all the constant questioning I did in my growing up years, it was not something I questioned.

It wasn't until I was an adult and had moved to the Western United States that I gained a whole new perspective on the indigenous peoples of this country. In a short time, my education went far beyond those early school teachings and the naïve ignorance of the majority of my adult life. In rapid succession, a whole new learning opened before my eyes. It would become a life-changing experience and one that continues to expand and grow... changing my thinking and my world.

Shortly after relocating to Colorado, I met a Cherokee Elder who was to become my mentor for over five years, leading me in exploring history through the wisdom of the First People. At this point my education into the true, rich meaning of Sacred Land began to form into reality. Black Tail Swan was willing to take me on as an apprentice and I happily opened my mind, heart and spirit to new knowledge.

I devoured every book I could get my hands on and explored the local Sacred Sites, such as the Southern Arapaho summer camp at Gold Lake in the Rocky Mountains, with Niwot, the peacemaker, as their chief to Sand Creek, out on the dry plains of eastern Colorado, where a brutal massacre killed women, children and Peace carrying Indians, including Niwot, who believed they were going to sign the final treaty.

> *As I stood looking over the land at Sand Creek, I could still feel the cries and see Earth Mother running red with blood of my brothers and sisters. The earth cried tears of loss and shame.*

The first lesson, when looking at indigenous people, is that every Native American Nation holds all of Earth Mother as Sacred. Think about the lifestyle of the indigenous peoples: they walked gently on the earth in bare feet or moccasins, neither leaves a scar on the land; they ate local vegetation or learned to grow crops that would become the basis of their diet; meat was gathered with reverence and great ceremony went into the preparation for the hunt. All parts of the animal were utilized and ceremony was again offered when the animal gave its life – no more animals were killed than were actually needed. All indigenous peoples hold in common that they live by honoring the seasons. Medicines came from the local plants which the Shaman were trained to use for healing. They walked with great respect for Earth Mother, caring for her and all her beings as one.

Mitakuye Oyasin – We are all Related.
It was Black Tail Swan who first told me about Denver Indian Market, held in January each year, and this is where my education expanded to include the many Indian Nations of the West. It was at Indian Market that I met Moses Brings Plenty, Oglala Lakota, from Pine Ridge Reservation. He was a childhood friend-of-a-friend of mine. Over the next few years, Moses helped to expand my world and knowledge. One year he asked me to go to Pine Ridge and help with the children. I promised him I would find a way to do that.

In the way of Great Spirit, within the next week a trip to the Pine Ridge Reservation was announced for the following summer through my church. It was to be a mission trip to do work on homes and with the children. This was what Moses had asked me to do, and yet, I still had so much more to learn. And so early in September 2008, I would walk on the Sacred Land of the Pine Ridge South Dakota Reservation, now home of the Oglala Lakota. Pine Ridge is the second largest and poorest of the Lakota Sioux Reservations. It covers over 11,000 square miles of some of the poorest soil in South Dakota.

History:
The Sioux were originally part of the Ojibwe/Chippewa/Asishinabe Nation, from the time when all of the Sioux lived closer to the mid-west (Wisconsin, Iowa, and Illinois) area. As the Sioux moved west, they broke away from this Nation, becoming known as the Mighty Sioux Nation as they moved out toward the plains. The Sioux included three language dialects: Lakota, Dakota and Nakota ("friends… allies… to be friendly"). Of the seven groups of Lakota, the Oglala are the largest.

The Western Sioux, the Lakota, consider the Black Hills of South Dakota their holiest home. To the Lakota, this 6000-square-mile area is the *heart of everything that is*. For the Lakota, *Tatanka*, the buffalo, came to the Lakota people from the Black Hills; this is part of their creation story. Buffalo came to provide the people with food and warmth. The story of *Tatanka* has been handed down the generations through their oral history. As the legend goes, the Great Spirit *Skan*, who grew out of Stone after the creation of Earth Mother, created all Lakota Ancestors. They were warmed by the sun, given wisdom through oral history and discovered affection for all through the light of the moon. It was a council of the Spirits who decided the purpose of the Lakota, which is to respect and care for the Spirits. At this council they were given their name: Buffalo Nation.

For a time the Buffalo Nation lived in the underworld, but coaxed by Wolf, one strong young man, Tokaka, believed that life would be easy on the surface of Earth Mother. A passage was discovered to the Black Hills through Wind Cave. For the people, life on Earth Mother was hard, but *Tatanka*, who had remained in the Underworld, saw this in a vision. And so, *Tatanka*, the buffalo, came to Earth as the great shaggy beast. *Tatanka* could speak directly with the Spirits. He came to willingly give his life so the Lakota people could have food, shelter and clothing. And so the Lakota lived with the buffalo in the land around the Black Hills peacefully from the beginning.

All remained peaceful until the white man wanted more and more land. With the greed of invaders, they felt this land was theirs to take; yet to the Lakota, the land belongs to no one; it is for all to care for and share.

In the beginning of the migration of the whites to the West, the Indian Nations tried to adjust and accommodate. As happens in humankind, that didn't always work and the great Sioux Nation found itself being squeezed into a smaller and smaller space. Treaties were signed and broken. More treaties were signed and broken.

The year was 1868; the treaty council at Fort Laramie, Wyoming had established the Great Sioux Nation Reservation. The original boundaries included about half of what is now South Dakota, including the 6000 acres of the sacred Black Hills, with a small corner of Nebraska. This area included the Lakota's Sacred Black Hills. And all was at peace until....

When gold was discovered in the Black Hills region in 1874, the federal government tried to buy back the Black Hills. This idea was inconceivable to the Sioux, after all, it was the birth place of their nation; but in 1877, Congress passed an act appropriating the land. Even after this matter has traveled through the courts, the Black Hills still remain outside of Lakota territory. The people continue to feel stripped of their roots and can not be whole until the Sacred Black Hills area has been returned.

Today, with twisted land grants, South Dakota has become sprinkled with ten reservations, covering perhaps 1/3 of the state. Each is littered with land that is mostly unusable and has little or no access to secure water sources or transportation services. The land is of little value for farming, and there is no infra-structure for employment and growth (unemployment consistently hovers at 80%).

In early 1890, the Paiute Indians in Nevada saw the sky darken (known today as a solar eclipse) and a Paiute Holy Man was taken to heaven. With his return, he told the Paiute that they could hasten to paradise through a special dance which became known as Ghost Dance. This was to be a dance of Sacred Peace. But the whites did not look at the context and assumed it would turn hostile. The Ghost Dance was said to connect the dancers with their departed relatives. A delegation of Oglala from the Pine Ridge Reservation was sent across the Rocky Mountains to investigate this new dance.

They returned in the spring of 1890 with a version which was adapted by the Lakota. With their deep spiritual tradition of communing with the Great Spirit through music and dance, the Lakota version included preliminary purification rites, in their ceremony custom. Additionally, dance leaders preached that the Ghost Dance was open to men, women and children in order to fulfill the promise of an Indian paradise in the next world. Through the dancing, the Lakota believed that Creator would eliminate white men from the face of the earth (however, it was never their intention to in any way contribute to the white man's destruction, just to have them relocate back to wherever they came from). The Oglala Ghost Dancers wore a decorated garment they called the Ghost Shirt. This was thought to protect them from physical harm.

Kicking Bear, Oglala Lakota, had gone to Standing Rock Reservation in October at the invitation of Sitting Bull, Hunkpapa Lakota, to share information about the Ghost Dance. Federal agents forced Kicking Bear to leave, but he had already been able to meet with many of the Hunkpapas.

> *My brothers,*
> *I bring you the promise of a day in which there will be no white man*
> *to lay his hand on the bridle of the Indian's horse,*
> *when the red men of the prairie will rule the world.*
> *I bring you word from your fathers the ghosts,*
> *that they are now marching to join you,*
> *led by the Messiah who came once to live on earth with the white man,*
> *but was cast out and killed by them.*

−KICKING BEAR, HUNKPAPA LAKOTA

The Ghost Dance as outlined by Kicking Bear provided a solution for the Lakota's most pressing issues. By eliminating the onslaught of white man through Divine intervention, life on the plains could return to the Peace and Tranquility that had been known for generations.

By late 1890, some 20,000 Lakota from four Dakota reservations were fervently taking up the Ghost Dance, including men, women and children, waiting for the day of reckoning which they expected to take place in the spring of 1891. The lines of the Ghost Dance had become a religious experience. As more and more Tribes of the Lakota Nation gathered, the Federal Army, concerned about an uprising, increased its forces.

And so it was, the Miniconjou Lakota, Ghost Dancers from Cheyenne River Reservation were gathered near a creek named Wounded Knee in a village on the Pine Ridge Reservation, seeking refuge and protection, not realizing that the army was gathering in larger and larger numbers. The dances began to attract the attention of white squatters living in the village as early as mid-September. The squatters demanded protection from the Ghost Dancers, resulting in even more troops being gathered. When the Miniconjou learned of Sitting Bull's death, they sought counsel with the army leader Colonel Sumner and requested safe passage back to their home reservation. It was agreed and they were preparing to leave.

No one will ever know for sure what happened that morning. On 29 December 1890, the Miniconjou had surrendered and were leaving, the white flag of peace flying. The atmosphere was charged and all it took was the firing of one gun to result in a full scale Indian massacre. The killing of Indian men, women and children numbered over 350. Of these, 200 were women and children. One woman who survived stated, "We tried to run, but they shot us like we were buffalo."

> *Something else died there in the bloody mud,*
> *and was buried in the blizzard,*
> *a people's dream died there.*

—BLACK ELK, SIOUX HOLY MAN

3 September 2009 Pine Ridge South Dakota

We were a small group of curious students, invited to journey to Wounded Knee to hear Story from Kelly Looking Horse, Oglala Lakota. It was a ten mile drive from where we were staying in the town of Pine Ridge. At that point, I had completed enough mentoring and studies to become accustomed to feeling energies from many sources.

Nothing prepared me for the wall of horror as we turned the corner to the mound that is Wounded Knee. Earth Mother remains alive with the pain and agony. The winds have continued to cry. And although it was a warm, still sunny late afternoon, my body was frozen with bone-chilling pains. The Earth rattled.

As Kelly Looking Horse relayed the story of the events that took place in the slow quiet Indian way, that echoes the voices of generations past, the pain of the Ancestors remained vivid and Earth Mother shook with her continuing tears.

We learned that on the morning of 3 January 1891, the army led a civilian burial party. Close to 150 bodies were interred in a mass grave, though many more lay where they fell in the frozen, snow covered ground. It was a dark day as we lined up, silently surrounding that mass grave. Kelly honored the fallen with prayer and tobacco and we each sprinkled our tobacco silently with our personal blessings.

We were given time for quiet meditation to wander the site of the mass grave, where bodies were cruelly dumped into a common grave, and the graves of others added later... So many children and women... Earth Mother runs red. This is Sacred Earth for all eternity.

A week later when I had completed my mission time I traveled further with a friend, a rancher's daughter, who grew up just north of Pine Ridge. A native of South Dakota, she knows the Badlands intimately. Her Story brings them to life with the mystery that they continue to hold, along with the buffalo that wander this barren land. We drove together to the Black Hills, to what is now called Wind Cave National Park.

Again I felt the energies of the Sacred Earth as we walked quietly to the opening in the Earth called Wind Cave, where *Tatanka*, the holy man who took the body of the buffalo, warned the Lakota people not to go to the surface. The temperature had climbed to 100 degrees that afternoon. There was no relief from the heat, or the hellish grief I experienced there. In the silence of personal meditation, I felt the visitation of the Ancestors. "It is all as it is meant to be," I heard them say. Is life truly so simple? Are we the ones who always try to make it so complex? It is a question with no answer.

My friend/mentor and beloved elder Arthur Short Bull, Oglala Lakota, reminds me that "Everything the Indian does is preceded by prayer and ceremony." He also assures me that the Indian are taking a stand and returning to their Indian ways… to walking on the Sacred Earth and feeling the Mother speak, hearing the Elders and honoring the Red Way. A Ho.

Back in Colorado, I often walked in the Rocky Mountains and felt the Native Spirits speaking in the wind. The Ute Indians were native to the area, and following the Ute trail in Rocky Mountain National Park brought Ancestral voices to my ears. I felt them walking with me, sharing Story as we walked together.

And now as I explore my new home in Western North Carolina, I feel the energies of the Cherokee encouraging me to walk a little further on the Red Road. In the words of the Lakota: "*Mitakuye Oyasin*" – we are all related. And so, when we harm one, we harm all. When we hurt Earth Mother in one location we hurt her everywhere. Let us all set the goal to bring Peace and Balance to this Sacred Earth in our lifetime. Hear her whisper. She is calling to you.

The Journey

The journey ahead is filled with light.

Life is a journey of turning cycles, spiraling ever higher. Enjoy this journey! Everything comes to those who prepare, listen and wait. In the whispers of spirit in the land, help is always available. Nearing arrival at our destination, we celebrate, knowing the rewards of our journey will be great.

Walking Sacred Earth
Pine Ridge was not the first time I have walked on the Sacred Earth of the Mother. I believe that every step I take is on Sacred Earth.

As a child, I was fortunate to grow up in the country, in a valley that was surrounded by the mountains of the Northern Appalachian Mountain chain. The Appalachian are said to be the oldest mountains in the world and I've always held them in both great respect and as my personal playground.

As a teen, a girlfriend and I would climb the mountain across from our homes nearly every evening. We'd carefully pack our dinner ingredients before leaving home, climb on a trail we had forged, often discussing the Lenape footsteps we were walking in. Our campfire pit was nestled in a spot near the mountain top in an area we had cleared.

As we gathered wood for our fire, we were careful not to disturb what was not dried and ready to burn and not to take more than we needed. Dinner always tasted more delicious when cooked over our sacred fire in our personal Sacred Site. We often felt the wisp of breeze, the gentle touch of a Lenape Elder, smiling at our honoring of Earth Mother and our forefathers who had walked before.

In today's world, those trails can be difficult to forge, but woodlands anywhere can create similar magic when shared with like-minded company. Bring the reality of your sacred honoring of Earth Mother from your heart and she will always show up.

I believe that Earth Mother considers each of us, including all: two-leggeds, four-leggeds, wigglers, diggers, and wingeds, as her Sacred Children. As such it becomes the responsibility of each of us to treat her with Love and Respect.

A great way to begin your journey of Walking Sacred Earth is through meditation. Music is helpful to accompany times of meditation; my favorite is the Native American flute music of Marina Raye. Her music can lead you on personal meditation journey to sacred earth as you listen and float with her melodious flute and the quiet sounds of nature in the background. As you sit in quiet meditation, you discover the touch of energies, the gentle nudge of awakening to the sense of being brushed by the knowledge that life is special, and that there are many locations where you can feel the gathering of the Sacred at work.

Go for a wander in Mother Nature. Sit quietly in a place where you can rest your back against a tree. Breathe deeply and slowly; let your eyes rest. Feel the warmth of the sun on your skin, smell Earth Mother, and feel her. Witness the richness of the growing plants around you. Perhaps there is a bird flying above; hear its call and feel the clouds moving slowly across the sky. Close your eyes and breathe all of this in. This is the Sacred Earth Mother. Listen to her; she will be happy to talk to you – always.

Another way to feel and understand the Sacredness of locations is to visit *designated* Sacred Sites. They are everywhere and anywhere; tours abound, both locally and abroad. A wonderful book on the journeys of a mother and daughter to Sacred Sites in Greece and France is *Traveling with Pomegranates* by Sue Monk Kidd and Ann Kidd Taylor. I thoroughly enjoyed the Unabridged CD reading by the authors. You hear the energy that explodes and expands for each as they walk the Sacred, then revisit and walk again with different feelings. You will hear how different experiences speak to each of them and how they individually and together grow.

And then again, there is the magic of discovering that no one needs to designate a site to be Sacred for it to be so. There are many locations in the world that are private Sacred Sites for me. Perhaps they are for others also, but all are without designation. I can feel the Sacred of Earth Mother as I sit by a stream, rest in a quiet meadow that appears in a forest, hear the sound of a waterfall talking, or listen to the rocks and trees – ask what messages they have to share with you.

Here in Western North Carolina, I have been fortunate to find another magical stream who gurgles and bubbles with laughter through every season. The beautiful boulders of Earth Mother hold space for Sacred Ceremony to be completed, either with others or privately.

Explore, you will soon begin to discover your own private Sacred Places, as you listen they will reveal themselves to you, as you become more and more in tune with hearing and feeling Earth Mother, remaining open to her revelations!

☙

DENICE MARTIN
Tootgarook, VIC, Australia

DENICE MARTIN IS A gifted medium and intuitive clairvoyant healer who works with the angelic and spiritual realm. She has studied at a number of Universities in education, poetry, Shakespeare, Italian, French and Japanese Haiku, obtaining a Graduate Certificate in Fraud Investigation at La Trobe University in Melbourne, having worked in this field since 1997.

She began her own business in the spiritual realm in early 2006 and travels frequently to explore as much of this world as she can. Denice's gift has been with her from early childhood although as a youngster only spoke of it with her paternal grandmother, from whom she inherited this gift, which developed further after her grandmother passed. She has three grown children of whom two are also gifted in this way and two granddaughters, one who has already displayed obvious signs of spiritual conversations.

Denice is a published author and poet, contributing to *Angels – Winged Whispers* and has works published on BlueThumbnail.com, in the upcoming *A Kink in My Armour*, as well as her own Inspiration Cards. She is an inspiring person who leads others with direction and confidence and states this is more fulfilling than anything else she could achieve on her own. Denice attributes her successes to those from the Angelic realm who channel their guidance and wisdom directly through her and onto the pages as she writes.

If you would like to experience a private consultation please contact Denice directly:

www.rainbowangel.vpweb.com.au
or email her at: rainbow_angel@y7mail.com

My Balinese Angel

DENICE MARTIN

*Some of the youngest children had been found wandering the streets alone.
It was strangers who had brought them here to the orphanage at Ubud.*

I awoke to another hot and steamy day in Bali. From the balcony of the resort, I could hear street noises, the typical hustle and bustle of these beautiful people going about their day's work. With my tea in hand, I leaned on the wooden rail overlooking a magnificent bunch of palm trees, some taller than my third floor room. I felt much anticipation and excitement as my thoughts turned to what the day ahead might bring.

Before leaving Melbourne for this road I have traveled many times, I had expectations that I now wanted to fulfill. Above all, I wanted to find an orphanage, since my mission involved a plan to make some quilts for the children. I also intended to sponsor one of these children for their education, until the age of eighteen. Firstly though, I needed to locate an orphanage. But before I could do anything, I needed to get a translation for the word *orphanage*!

After my two friends had woken, we headed out for breakfast at a familiar cafe. As Wayan, our waitress, took our order, we asked her if she knew the whereabouts of an orphanage. She couldn't quite understand what we wanted, and after some confusion, we decided to let her continue making our breakfast and we would try again later.

As I was enjoying my delicious breakfast of French toast followed by an icy cold fresh orange juice, I noticed that seated at the next table was an Australian couple with their young son. We all got talking, as you do when on holiday. Apparently we were all from Melbourne, so there was much chatter between us as we shared some of our favorite Balinese places. They mentioned that they had been to the town of Ubud some days earlier and had passed an orphanage there, but couldn't quite remember where it was. At least this was a starting point; so off we headed.

We located a taxi and informed the driver that we wanted to go to Ubud and that we may wish to stop along the way. After driving for about forty-five minutes, we came across an art gallery. Both Kira and I love art and made our way inside while Coz and our taxi driver remained outside to chat with the locals. The gallery contained some amazing art works, housed in individual rooms according to theme. The gallery owner giggled to himself as we waltzed quickly through a whole room based on the Karma Sutra.

As we entered a room containing paintings of local women and children, I found myself being drawn to a portrait of a woman nursing a baby wrapped in silk cloth. The emotion in the woman's face had been captured in great detail by the artist's brushstrokes, and she appeared distressed. The pain in her eyes told a whole story in itself. Putting myself in this mother's position, I wondered about the story behind such a painting.

I stood for a long time taking some photos of this piece. Then, just as I was putting my camera away, a strange sensation came over me. I know this feeling well as a change in my vibration like this always occurs when spirit is near. I noticed, standing just below this large painting, the spirit of a young child.

As I am clairvoyant, I could see her quite clearly as she gazed into the picture mesmerized. I kept quite still so as not to disturb her but wanted to communicate with this spirit. With that intention, I set my thoughts towards making contact. Her name was Lila and although she didn't look at me, she was well aware of my presence and we were able to communicate quite easily. I asked what brought her here today and she told me she loved the woman in this painting, which had special significance to her. I asked her to please tell me more.

The artist completed this painting at the request of his sister. She had given birth to five children over a number of years and this baby was the youngest and last born. This infant was dying from pneumonia but the mother could do nothing now, as the illness was progressing rapidly. She was saying her goodbyes, so sad that this lovely little girl was leaving her after such a short a time.

There were some wooden chairs in the middle of the gallery so I sat down and beckoned for Lila to join me. I wanted to know more about her and why she was here, so I questioned her silently as we sat together.

She explained that she was in fact the little baby in the painting, and that it was now her task in the spirit world to look after the little babies once they had crossed over from the living world, to what is so often referred to as Heaven. She wanted to know why I was so taken with the painting of her mother. I told her that I have a love of art, especially paintings with vibrant colours such as this one.

But as I kept looking at the painting, while I was explaining myself to Lila, I suddenly began to see specific items in the picture that I hadn't noticed before. In this painting, the mother and baby were seated on a bed surrounded by soft, colorful cushions. The bed was a traditional open bed with just a mattress on top. There were no blankets covering this bed, only cushions. Lila informed me that the white, silk cloth she was wrapped in, edged with very old lace, had been hand sewn by her grandmother and blessed by the family. She had been wrapped by her parents in this beautiful fabric for her burial.

I asked her how she felt now, seeing everything from the angelic world in which she now lived. Lila told me that she wasn't sad because she could curl up in her mother's arms at any time. Although her mother couldn't feel her physically, Lila could feel her mother. She knew that her mother sensed when she was near, as she would begin to smile, and her heart would brim with love. The soul can communicate with any other soul, though the physical body may not be aware of this. This feeling of love stayed with Lila from the moment of her birth. She explained that the emotional bond between a mother and child never dies. The soul goes on living and feeling, because it is just the physical body which ceases to exist.

Whenever her mother thought of Lila, the thought seemed to travel to wherever Lila was. Lila would immediately appear beside her mother to help comfort her, moving so close with her spiritual body that her mother would calm down straight away. It was as if they could communicate telepathically, but Lila knew it was her soul speaking directly with her mother's soul. She loved this part of her spiritual life because this bond could never be broken by anything or anyone. Lila said that whenever a baby passed over into the spirit world, they could return quite easily to soothe and comfort their mother's soul, and that this comfort was surely felt and had wonderful healing qualities for them both.

I was comforted by the thought that Lila was happy with her spiritual home and life. And since I had lost two babies of my own, I felt a sense of calm come over me with the knowledge that my babies could arrive by my side in an instant, whenever I thought of them.

Though my babies, a boy and a girl, passed a few years apart, I knew that they were together and often visited me. Like many clairvoyants, I can see quite clearly for other people, though when it comes to myself, I only sense things.

Lila told me she could see my two babies with me as we spoke. While we were talking about the bond between a mother and child, I had experienced sadness for my own loss. My babies must have sensed this and now appeared, exactly as Lila had described. Just thinking about them drew them to my side in an instant. I smiled inside and felt tears welling in my eyes as I sensed my babies close to my chest. Lila knew what I was feeling. She told me that if I closed my eyes I would see them clearly. When I closed my eyes, it felt as though I was being transported up a long grassy field, and in each arm I held my babies.

There was no weight, nor did I feel tired. It felt as if I was floating. As I reached the top of the hill, I saw a magnificent old oak tree. Its branches were large and wide and seemed to extend far away from the trunk of the tree, each branch completely covered with leaves. I sat with my babies on the grass under this beautiful tree. I felt as though I should name them, and the first names to pop into my head were Timothy and Claire. Timothy was running around me in tight little circles, laughing and giggling to himself. He was full of life, happy and bursting with energy. Claire on the other hand sat on my lap, her back resting against me. I could see her smiling and knew that she was happy and at peace too. And when I stared into her eyes, I knew I was at home.

Though I had lost both babies very early in my pregnancies, I could now see them as they would appear as they grew older. Timothy seemed to be around the age of four, while Claire was two. I imagined myself giving them both a kiss and a hug as they left my side. A deep sense of peace washed over me. I felt my heart swell within my chest and was now glowing inside. I opened my eyes.

Lila impressed on me that it was now time for her to go. I felt a little sad as I had enjoyed our time together and what she had shown me. She knew what I was thinking and told me that she would see me again soon. I wondered what she meant by this and pondered the thought.

It seemed I had been gone for at least half and hour, so I now moved quickly through the rest of the art gallery looking for Kira. As I located her, I apologized for being away so long and delaying our trip. She said I had only been gone a few minutes. I reminded myself once again that time is very different in the spiritual world.

We raced outside to find Coz who was still chatting with the locals, then jumped into our taxi and headed further into Ubud. The taxi driver dropped us off at the Monkey Forest, located at the beginning of the main shopping district. We meandered along this gorgeous little rustic town, speaking with many of the locals as they went about their business. We made our way through the markets, enjoying the banter of the locals as they tried to barter with us to buy their goods.

I purchased an unusual Balinese musical instrument from the market which was carved from a large coconut. It was hand painted with small metal pieces above a hole carved into it. Similar to a guitar, you pluck the metal pieces to make the most beautiful sound. We bought many things we didn't really need, but it made us feel good to help the people of the village with their financial needs.

It had become quite hot and steamy and then the rains came, so everyone charged under a covered area. This made the markets humid and stuffy, so we decided to end our shopping expedition and head out into the surrounding streets of Ubud to look for our orphanage.

The taxi driver took us along some very windy roads and soon we passed a procession of local people, all dressed in national costume. We asked what event could be happening and the driver told us that they were going to a wedding, a family wedding. We were very excited to see this group of happy people expressing the love of a family which was about to grow and join another, to become much larger.

Our taxi came to a halt in front of a yellow building which was no bigger than a small shop. This was the orphanage and school of Ubud. It was called *Yayasan Widya Guna* or in English, 'The Foundation of the Children's Education.' We entered into what was obviously a classroom, as there were rows of school desks and lots of books sitting in a large pile on top of a table. Hearing the sound of children playing out the back, we headed in their direction looking for an adult.

A group of six children of varying ages ran up to us and started speaking to us in English. Their English was excellent, so we knew they had been tutored by an English teacher at some stage. We asked for a teacher and a couple of children ran off to fetch him. The teacher's name was Nyorman and when he arrived, he showed us through the whole orphanage. He explained that it held one hundred children, of which only about nine slept there because they had nowhere else to live, no parents or family. All the other children went home at the end of the school day which was shortly after lunch. They only came to the school to be cared for, fed and educated. Some of the youngest children had been found wandering the streets alone. It was strangers who had brought them here to the orphanage at Ubud.

Nyorman explained that many sponsors came from all over the world to offer financial support for the education of these little ones. Apparently, for the sum of only a few dollars a month, a child could complete their entire Secondary education. A few could go onto University if they chose. They already had one pupil studying to be a doctor and another to be a lawyer, which made them all very proud. As we continued on our tour, we learnt all about this wonderful and secluded oasis.

The children ran and played around us while we chatted and learned the history of this family and school, which was surrounded by a huge brick and timber wall, making it appear like a small community within a community.

Passing through the school house, we came into a courtyard surrounded by other buildings. Here there was a garden which was overflowing with an abundance of fresh vegetables and herbs. Some of the vegetables we knew well like potatoes, lettuce and tomatoes and some were quite unfamiliar.

Here we met Nyorman's mother. Her name was Sudra for she is from a family of rice growers. Sudra is a tiny woman with long black hair pulled back from her happy, smiling face in a neat little bun. When she came over to greet us, the children all buzzed around her happily, as if she were their own mother. It was such a beautiful sight to see. These children who had lived such a basic life, with very few commodities, looked so happy! Their cute little faces brimmed with joy and love. Just looking at their smiles from ear to ear, made you feel happy to be alive. We felt so privileged to visit such a place.

Hope

The flame of hope glows within my heart.

The laughter of children ignites inspiration, enthusiasm and hope, the way flashes of lightning bring creative energy and nourishment to the earth. By announcing our intentions and remaining open, resources appear. Our inspiration becomes contagious, opening the way forward with hope.

You see, this orphanage is Nyorman's family home which his mother had allowed him to open as a school and orphanage, for the sake of the children who live within this small community. It was wonderful to listen to Nyorman and his dreams of opening his own orphanage one day. He had already been able to secure some land a short distance from his mother's home. He was now looking for funding to complete the project of building a sizeable new home and orphanage, which would cater for many more children. We listened excitedly as he spoke of his dream, which we felt sure would soon become a reality.

We were very impressed to be shown the music room which was filled with musical instruments played by the children. It contained beautiful brass instruments, similar to a xylophone but on a much bigger scale. There were also three guitars, a drum set and some symbols. We learned that most of the funds to run the school were raised through musical concerts performed by the children of the orphanage.

As it was nearing time to say our goodbyes, Nyorman and one of the volunteers said the children wanted to perform a song for us. We were delighted! While the children began to gather in a central area of the garden, I noticed that Lila had come to join us. Now I knew what she had meant when she said she would be seeing me soon. She loved to be with these children because they could see her, and they all played along with her. She felt a sense of peace here. She was able to provide comfort to any of the children who cried when they went to bed, making them feel peaceful and secure.

The children now began to sing a song in perfect English, called 'You Are My Sunshine.' Tears welled up in our eyes as they sang. It was so beautiful to hear them. We were absolutely sobbing now, and turned to leave. But the children all called out that they had another song to sing for us. This one was called 'My Flower' and was sung to us in Balinese. They sang this song three times, once for each of us, using each of our names with each new rendition. We felt so loved, as though every child there loved us unconditionally. It was the most amazing feeling. Our hearts filled to overflowing with the same amount of love, returning it to these beautiful children.

There was nothing more to say. We felt blessed to have experienced such love coming from children who were quite poor, but who were so rich in love.

We left, explaining to Nyorman and his mother that we would return soon with a few things for the children. We drove off and soon located a General Store on the outskirts of this little community. We searched for colored pencils, lead pencils with erasers, exercise books, rulers, felt pens and also a ten kilo bag of rice. We all had so much fun shopping at this rustic little store! Actually, none of us had felt such pleasure as we did when we arrived back at the orphanage and handed over the supplies. Nyorman and his mother were overwhelmed at our generosity, but it was the three of us who felt we were the ones who had received the most amazing gift that day. We were filled with delight at the generosity of the children and for Nyorman and his mother in sharing with us their beautiful oasis, their family home.

The children walked us back to our taxi and as we drove away, they ran after us waving and blowing kisses. The three of us – well traveled, confident, career girls – were like putty in their hands, totally taken over by the emotion of the day. Through my blessed happy tears, I watched as Lila ran and laughed with all the other children, so totally oblivious to the fact that she was not in physical form. The children playing with her did not see her as anything other than another child of the little Balinese orphanage.

Connecting with your Loved One

I would like to teach you how to connect with someone who has already passed over. All you will need is a few basic steps to take you to the next level of vibration, so that you can truly feel the difference when spirit comes near.

Move to a place where you can relax totally, without any disturbances. It doesn't matter whether this is inside, outside, day or night. An ideal place might be sitting on the grass outside on a sunny day. It is completely up to you where you feel most comfortable and relaxed.

Now light a candle, either scented or unscented. Sit in a comfortable position with your legs uncrossed. This could be on a couch, arm chair or even sitting on your bed propped up with some pillows.

Take in three deep breaths and as you exhale, blow all of the breath out of your body, slowly and deeply. Whilst you do this, imagine that with every exhaled breath, any worries, stress or concerns are leaving your body. These concerns and worries will be captured gently by your angels and dispersed.

As you finish exhaling, move your awareness into your heart. Feel the beat of your heart as it is slowing down to enjoy a beautiful healing energy which is now surrounding your body, and moving throughout every single part without any blockages or interruptions.

Imagine this energy to be like rainbow colours as it swirls inside you and connects with every organ. Don't let any other thoughts pop into your mind. If they do, just take your mind back to this lovely rainbow energy.

Now imagine that you are the nerve centers of your skin, and can feel everything which touches you, from the air molecules you breathe, to the tiny dust particles which travel around you. Clear your mind and as you do, keeping your thoughts solely on your skin.

Hold the intention that you wish to meet with that someone special with whom you share a connection. As you do this, take your mind now to your arms, and the skin around them. Feel a change coming around every part of your body, but especially your arms. Do you feel a tingle or perhaps a slight breath of wind, so slight that you may think a butterfly is moving within your aura? Breathe in and out, as slowly as you can.

Move your focus to your third eye. Open it and see this clear third eye, noticing each and every eyelash. With your mind, imagine wiping away any visionary area you feel is blurred.

You will see someone moving closer to you from a distance away. Imagine holding out your arms toward this spirit and welcoming them to join you. Feel the change in your skin and notice any heightened feelings or sensitivities.

Once your loved one is close to you, so close you will feel your aura or the vibration around your whole body change, you will be able to recognize this person whom you so wanted to see. Sit with them and look into their eyes. Listen to what thoughts pop into your head, making a mental note to worry about the details later.

How do you feel? Do you feel happy, fulfilled, loved, overjoyed, or perhaps a little sad? Now that you are conversing with your loved one, feel the message this person is trying to convey. Don't judge or think that what you are hearing is your own imagination because it is not; it is truly from spirit.

You will know when it is time to say goodbye. If you have not yet said everything that you wanted them to hear, tell them now. They can hear you just as you can hear them now. Feel their energy around your body, and as they begin to move away, notice the difference in your body, the feel of your skin, your aura and your emotions.

Now see the rainbow energy appear once again, surrounding your body with the true healing energy of spirit. Imagine the swirls of colour as this energy protects you, sealing your whole body with pure love. Feel the change in yourself as you return to your normal, daily time. You are now more relaxed than ever, feeling deeply rested.

What you have experienced is a very personal thing. It is very different for every individual, depending on our level of consciousness. You may revisit this experience at any time of day or night. All you need is the intention.

It is a great idea afterwards to write a journal, keeping detailed notes of your experiences so that you can then make comparisons each time you do this.

Once you experience the difference in your own vibration, you will truly know that you have indeed experienced a visit from your loved one.

Abundance

I am grateful, for everything.

We give thanks for the bounty of abundance being poured down upon us through countless blessings. Noticing that we have more than enough to be content, we give freely where it is needed. This only increases our joy, and our abundance.

JP AMES
Westminster, Colorado USA

FROM SEA TO SHINING SEA, JP's travels on this planet have encompassed the mainland USA, with several flights across the ocean to the beautiful 50th state, Hawaii. Her main venture outside of the USA has been a Norwegian Cruise which allowed passengers the opportunity to visit Fanning Island, in the Republic of Kiribati. These planet ventures have brought JP to the edge, to explore and discover more fully the beauty of the land. Each journey has expanded her self-awareness and her appreciation for this glorious planet which provides all life forms the ability to live and thrive.

Reviewing her outings, JP noticed the common thread of these adventures bringing her to the Water's Edge. The element of water has unconsciously been present to and for her in times of great distress, as well as in times of blissful joy. As a spiritual seeker, JP has found herself leaving home and living on the edge of many ventures/experiences awakening a deeper connection and meaning to the sacredness of her life. In the quest for answers and finding that sense of belonging, she found herself striving endlessly at the edge, looking outside herself for answers. Having come full circle, she now becomes quiet and listens from within to seek and find peace and knowingness that is her truth while living at the "Water's Edge."

JP is certified in Soul Coaching® and Past Life Regression and can be contacted at – jpcandoit@mac.com.

Water's Edge

JP AMES

I was brought to the Water's Edge to discover a glorious oasis of land which overcame adversity through goodwill and grace.

istening to the relaxing sounds of the 'Ocean Surf' playing in the background, I gaze through my window, beyond the trees and mountains, finding comfort as I raise my eyes to the sky. Though land-locked, I imagine this blue sky to be the majestic ocean, and the billowing white clouds passing overhead to be powerful surging waves. Becoming totally and completely immersed in the imagery, I ask myself: Why am I so drawn to the ocean waters when the fear of water runs so deep within my being?

As a child, all attempts at swimming lessons and the sure fire 'fear cure' of being tossed into the river failed. I know too well the feeling of gasping for air and drinking water frightfully. Yet, when enrolling my children for swimming lessons, I too enrolled. While swimming laps, I felt 100% in the *now*, every cell of my body focused on the stroke and breathing pattern, to sustain me to the other end of the pool.

Once out of the pool and going about my day, I felt refreshed and peaceful. It was as though the waters had cleansed my thoughts, words and actions. To this day, I have a very deep and humble respect and caution for water. Still, when seeming disaster strikes or raging thoughts overpower my very being – peace and calm return to me through the imagery of the ocean surf. I go to the Water's Edge, inhaling through all of my senses the soothing sounds of the cresting waves, the call of birds in flight, the sea breeze draping my form as it flows past, leaving an invisible mist of salt upon me. It is as if I become one with the pulsating rhythm of the moving, changing, flowing waves and the water-soaked sand that sinks beneath my bare feet, receding with the tide. Time has passed…

It was mid-June of 2004 when I packed my car and headed out from Arvada, Colorado. My first stop was just 50 miles north in Fort Collins, Colorado. It was a significant visit with a very close friend. As we reconnected, the true reason for this journey – to be physically reunited with family and old friends – surfaced. Actually, the trip was my way of bringing closure to my life, as I strategically planned ways to ease the pain of living. It would be the farewell before quietly and graciously following through with a self-imposed exit from this planet, which seemed deafeningly silent to my existence at that moment.

These totally devastating feelings were triggered after receiving a spiritual 'two-by-four' blow to the side of the head. I was unexpectedly laid off by the religious organization I worked for. This was the job I had prayed for and I had thought was the answer to my prayers. Yet God had other ideas. Needless to say, in my abounding self-pity, many a tear fell. My heart was heavy; everything about me was heavy. The voices of self-destruction reverberated explosively, venomously inside my head.

However, as I sniffled and wiped the tears away, I began reading *The Secret of Letting Go* by Guy Finley. His message stirred me into action. I discovered he was offering a June seminar in Merlin, Oregon. Even though I told myself that the plan to end it all was the reason behind my travel plans, I noticed that I was beginning to get excited about this trip. Since I was born and raised in Lebanon, Oregon, the door was opening to visit family and friends in person after an absence of 22 years. Since college, my life adventures had taken me to California, Hawaii, Texas and Mississippi, before settling down in Colorado.

I set out slowly to drive the more than 1,724 miles to Oregon, enjoying the sights and sounds along the way. I made it safely to my oldest brother's home in Albany, Oregon, where I was graciously hosted whilst visiting family and friends in nearby Lebanon. After being away for 22 years, the changes to the area were quite dramatic. So much so, that I was unable to recognize the turnoff to the last house I lived in. In spite of a few unsettling childhood memories surfacing, the visit with my siblings, nieces, nephews, and friends was timely and deeply cherished. After a week, with a slight detour to visit friends on the coast in Coos Bay, Oregon, I was off to the seminar in Merlin. This was scheduled to be my last stop before returning to Colorado, until...

I somehow learned that during World War II, the Japanese bombed Brookings, Oregon, so I decided to visit the bombsite. Up to this point, my entire road trip had been neatly planned and covered familiar territory. But now, the prospect of this solo journey into the unknown, outside my comfort zone, had my heart racing a bit. Yet deep within my soul, I knew without a doubt that I must go to this place, despite its limited highway access. Pioneer instincts kicked in and no matter what, I was on a mission to blaze a new trail!

Driving north on Highway 101, I became totally mesmerized by the unexpected beauty and majesty of this remote wonderland. The hills were alive with acres and acres of evergreen trees. Fields of white Easter Lilies by the roadside took my breath away. And as the blue ocean waves crested, rolling, flowing, receding and becoming one with the sandy shore, I felt as if I was driving into a magical fairyland, protected by the forest to the East and the ocean to the West.

Continuing north on Highway 101 and crossing over the Chetco River Bridge, the town of Brookings suddenly appeared. This idyllic coastal community, set in lush Southern Oregon, lies just six miles north of the California border. How could such a beautiful fertile area have been bombed? With wonderment in my heart, I located the Visitor's Information Center and received both information on the Japanese World War II bombing and directions to locate the bombsite in the National Forest. Well armed with the material necessary to blaze a new trail and explore as a pioneer this mountainous forest terrain, I read the narrative recounting the bombing …

It was just before dawn, September 9, 1942; a Japanese I-25 submarine surfaced 25 miles off Cape Blanco, Port Oxford, Oregon (north of Brookings). It was equipped with a watertight float plane hanger, holding a tiny modified zero. A catapult was used to launch the aircraft, with two 170lbs thermite incendiary bombs, into the air. Piloted by Warrant Officer Nubuo Fujita and his observer Shoji Okuda, the plane headed south. The first bomb was dropped over Wheeler Ridge, 16 miles east of Brookings. Officer Fujita saw an explosion, dropped the second bomb a few miles north and returned to the waiting sub.

Officer Fujita was treated as a hero in Japan. He did not know that his daring raid (in retaliation for Jimmy Doolittle's raid on Tokyo) fizzled because of an unusually early wet fall. The expected fires failed to ignite. The second bomb did not detonate. The Japanese plan was to "strike terror into the hearts of the American people" by starting devastating forest fires. The raid remains historically significant as the first time the US mainland had been bombed by enemy aircraft.

In 1962, the Brookings Junior Chamber of Commerce began a search for the pilot of this bombing raid to invite him as their guest to the local Azalea Festival. They hoped this gesture would help boost international goodwill.

An invitation was extended to Mr. Fujita and his family. Donations were sought and enough was received to finance their trip from Japan to Brookings. Mr. Fujita was greatly saddened to learn that his visit was considered controversial. He had become a pacifist and wanted only peace and understanding between the two countries. Despite continued threats to his safety, Mr. Fujita and his family were welcomed cordially by the residents of Brookings.

Mr. Fujita, with his son's consent, presented his family's 400-year-old Samurai sword to the City of Brookings. The sword had been with him on the raid in 1942, and throughout the war. It is in the finest of Samurai traditions to pledge peace and friendship by submitting the sword to a former enemy. This genuine act of contrition and friendship has truly made the sword "a gift of peace."

Later, on September 8, 1992, Mr. Fujita planted a coastal redwood at the bombsite. It was his apology to the forest. "I offer my deepest prayers now for the repose of all those who died in the war… but, I pray too for this commemorative tree of friendship, and for peace to live through hundreds of years, to grow into the tallest reflection of our mutual pledge for friendship and peace."

This area is now known as the Easter Lily Capital of the World. Prior to 1941, the majority of the Easter Lily bulbs were exported to the United States from Japan. World War II eliminated the dependence on Japanese-produced bulbs and commercial bulb production shifted to the US.

Today over 95% of all bulbs grown for the potted Easter Lily market are produced by just ten farms in a narrow coastal region straddling the California-Oregon border, from Smith River, California up to Brookings, Oregon.

For many, the beautiful trumpet-shaped white flowers symbolize purity, virtue, innocence, hope and life.

Closing the pamphlet, my emotions welled up. I gave thanks that the autumn of 1942 was unusually wet. I gave thanks that in 1962, the community reached out to extend "goodwill" to Mr. Fujita, the bomber pilot, and his family; and that in 1992 Mr. Fujita planted a commemorative coastal redwood tree of friendship – apologizing to the forest and offering prayers for all those who lost their lives during the war. How ironic that the Easter Lily bulb production shifted from Japan to the location they bombed during World War II, and that the plant with its trumpet-shaped white flowers symbolizes purity, innocence and hope.

Emotional Tides

I trust my innermost feelings.

To live in balance with the ebb and flow of our emotions, we can neither stem the tides of sadness nor of great joy. Feelings flow freely, allowing our true nature to shine. Accepting our true feelings, we risk slight changes in course, moving towards emotional replenishment, restoring our inner harmony.

This awareness shifted my journey from simply a random adventure taken out of curiosity, to a sacred quest. With map in hand, I drove to the forest road entrance that appeared to provide the fastest route. Within a short distance, ruts and crevices in the road brought me to an immediate stop. After surveying these deep ruts from every possible angle, I couldn't imagine continuing on this way. 'Option B', the longer route, quickly turned into the better choice. As a forging pioneer, I turned around, retracing the miles back to the main road to start over. Locating the first county graveled road, I entered the dense forestland, reading the map with one hand and trying not to look down over the steep precipice beside the road. There was no traffic at all on this 20-mile stretch. I drove along without a care in the world, in spite of the steep, narrow road, where at some points the treetops beside me were level with the road.

My car was doing well. But, according to the map, the trailhead should be right about here. I had said that a few times over the course of what seemed like hours. Finally, I began to wonder if I had somehow missed the sign for the trailhead. I wasn't sure whether I should turn around or continue on. All of a sudden there was a tree lying halfway across the road. I was able to maneuver around it, noticing beyond it, deep ruts and crevices that brought me to an abrupt stop. What now?

Once again I was confronted with a deeply rutted road that looked impassable from every angle. Options raced through my mind. How many hours had I been driving on these remote gravel roads? Several. Did I know where I was? Not really. But I had the map with the last recognizable intersection miles back. The narrow road plus the steep cliff edge ruled out turning the car around. I could walk out and get help somewhere, but this could take hours and it was nearly twilight. Or, I could risk calculating the wheelbase of the car with the width of the highest two ledges of the deep crevices, and go for it.

After a brief conversation with myself, I decided to be a circus daredevil racer and drive across the two 'high ledges' like two tight ropes, to the other side of the deeply rutted and creviced ravine. Did I pray? Yes! Did I close my eyes? No! Did I believe that I could do it? Yes! I took a deep breath and started the engine of the greatest car in the world! I put it in first gear, pressed down on the gas pedal gingerly and inched cautiously forward. Once I could feel all four tires on the ledges, I sped up just a little and made it across. I made an immediate Victory Stop, kissing the car, the ground, then lifting my eyes to the heavens to give thanks, ending with a victory dance singing "I made it! I made it! Thank You God! I made it!"

I had not visited the bombsite, but I had made it across a section of the road that appeared at first glance to be impossible to pass. I got into the car and started driving again, hoping to find some signs of life or a road mileage marker to help get my bearings. As I meandered down the road looking intently around, I suddenly realized I had been here before. I had gone full circle, crossing the section of the road I had said "No" to earlier that day. I laughed heartily for a good while. No, I never did find the bombsite, yet I believe the gift from this experience was more valuable.

Not all perceptions are true. I perceived at first that I was incapable of crossing the rutted creviced section of the road. Yet, in spite of myself, I safely made it over to the other side. All things are possible from the perspective of moving, changing and flowing with creation, and the blending of the seen and unseen, fostering the energetic flow of the unknown. I experienced this en route as I learned to trust and believe intuitively, moment-by-moment without question, that I would be able to deal with and size up the situation favorably. I was not alone, nor was I truly conscious of the vast number of guides from the invisible world that were by my side all the way.

The author Denise Linn often says "The Soul Loves the Truth." As I relive this road trip and the unexpected final destination, all I can say is that I felt at peace with the choices I made along the way, especially when I chose to venture into what was uncharted territory for me. From the moment I decided to move forward, I felt a knowing and a sense of safety and security in going through with the journey. My soul became my 'co-pilot.'

I'm learning that working with intuitive guidance is not as complicated as one might think. As Caroline Myss says, it is as simple as knowing whether you feel happy or not. I love that you don't have to eat tofu, remain in a headstand for twenty minutes, or a yoga posture for three hours in order to receive guidance. It is enough to relax, pay attention to what you are thinking and feeling, and to trust that your Divine Energy source is communicating with you.

Initially, I had planned to go to Brookings, locate the bombsite and leave the next day. However, as I moved, changed and flowed with the experience, the trek turned out quite different than I expected. It was as if I had been drawn to Brookings, Oregon by unconscious spiritual whispers. I was brought to the ocean Water's Edge and happened upon a glorious oasis of land that has overcome traumatizing adversity through goodwill and grace. I was filled with the magical energy of this charmingly simple, flourishing community, and my soul felt at home.

On the morning of my departure, I walked barefoot in the sand, witnessing the constant pulse of life with the rise and fall of the tide connecting rhythmically with the shore. Every cell in my body was enraptured by the billowing waves, receding water running over my feet, and the invisible sea breeze moving my clothing and flowing through my hair. Mesmerized by it all, I gazed beyond the Water's Edge and became immersed in the limitless blue horizon, unable to define where the ocean water ended and the heavenly sky began. It was as if time stopped and I was encapsulated in the moment, free and at one with the blending of the ocean and the sky. Blissfully, I moved with the energetic rhythm of the nurturing, sustaining, circulating Water's Edge. I felt totally and completely 100% in the *now*.

The experience of being drawn to Brookings, Oregon, was no accident. Divine Guidance was instrumental in planting the notion. When the idea first struck, I chose specifically, without a shadow of doubt, to follow this whimsical thought. Brookings called my soul because of its position on the coastline of the Pacific Ocean. It gave me the opportunity to venture to the Water's Edge, and to explore land that had been subjected to trauma and adversity.

On the road again and as the sites of Brookings faded out of sight, my mind became flooded with powerful symbolic impressions of what I had encountered during my unplanned trip to the Water's Edge. I had arrived at a beautiful, magical fairyland through a narrow, winding coastal highway, banked by magnificent redwood trees, overlooking the spectacularly scenic Pacific Ocean. My own life journey seems to be following a narrow, winding path, banked by magnificent challenges that at times have definitely shadowed the spectacular horizon of my walk. Here I was driving into two communities literally bridged together as one. Is not this life quest about bridging our tangible (created) world with our intangible (creative) world, striving to be both fully human and fully divine, perhaps even the instrument of spiritual wisdom through this human form?

This remote, pristine area was bombed during World War II. The incident was kept hush-hush and out of the press. My isolated, innocent childhood was overshadowed by being physically and emotionally mishandled and traumatized by adult males. These occasions were kept hush-hush, taking place in private over a number of years. Between the years of 1962 and 1995 the people of Brookings reunited with Mr. Fujita, the Japanese pilot who dropped WWII bombs here. Over the years, he took steps to heal the physical and emotional damage that had been done.

Similarly, over the course of my moving, changing and flowing with my life experiences, I have moved towards physical and emotional healing. It has been like a rebirthing – creating a loving environment where I felt safe, then opening up to the beauty surrounding me, ever remembering that I am not alone. The acts of letting go and finding forgiveness have been instrumental in the ebb and flow of this transition.

The final symbolic element of my journey that touched me deeply was the fields of Easter Lilies. This flower that prior to World War II was exported from Japan, is now flourishing in the area bombed by Japan. Here we have a unique, ideal combination of climate, soil, water and the human hand developing a product of deep meaning, beauty and tradition, identifying this area as – 'The Easter Lily Capital of the World.' In life, everything is possible when the ideal combination of faith, belief, acceptance, water, soul and the Infinite Life energy of Source come together to produce the meaningful, beautiful, creative expression of You, all human life forms, and Me.

In retrospect, I realize what a gift I was given, by my moving, changing and flowing with what I now know were planet whispers. Even though I began my journey emotionally despondent, feeling hopeless about going on, from the moment I began planning and actively making the trip happen, my shift in focus began to neutralize the initial thought patterns of self-imposed elimination. The whispers and nudges were subtle and yet profound as I now, years later, recount this life experience to you in my physical form. As I write, I am renewed with greater awe and gratitude for the ever flowing unconditional love and sustaining primal life source that permeates this entire planet, and all of it inhabitants.

It was planet whispers that called me to the Water's Edge. I was given the time that I needed to connect my soul more dynamically with the energy of the planet. It was a time of forgiveness and letting go, of being refreshed, and rejuvenated. Whenever I follow the whispered calls, I am consoled and rejuvenated from the inside out.

As the relaxing sounds of the 'Ocean Surf' stop playing in the background, I turn my gaze from the window, and once again ask myself: Why am I so drawn to the ocean waters when the fear of water runs deep within my being? In this moment, as if cleansed by a gentle wave, I realize that water is my deepest and dearest friend. I need to flow through the appearance of being afraid of water to the magnificent, energetic connection that my soul has with water. By doing this, the inner truth of my soul is free to flow and express through my every thought, word and action with greater ease and clarity. Those 100% in the *now* moments have the freedom to occur with the ebb and flow of my life experiences, rather than as a rare fleeting accident. The truth is I feel more grounded and flowing with my higher self when connected with the life energy source – water.

Standing at the ocean Water's Edge, I realize that I am not the expansive blending of the ocean water and the heavenly sky, yet I feel totally and completely immersed with the attributes of both when I become quiet within and listen.

Listen, listen, listen… and quietly hear the planet whispers stirring you and your soul into action.

Becoming Aware of how the Planet Whispers to Your Soul

Daily set aside time to acknowledge and nurture your soul. A few examples are: meditation, reading an uplifting book, listening to music, or through movement and dance.

Four Elements:
Spend time studying and becoming familiar with the four elements that represent the substance of planet earth – Water, Wind, Earth and Fire. Pay attention to the element that resonates most strongly with you and stirs your soul into action.

Movement:
Move, breathe and notice that with each movement, change and flow are engaged. The evolution of change is constant and profound, whether small or large. Through the movement, allow yourself to open up to new possibilities to hear and know your connection with Planet Whispers.

Time in Nature:
Venture forth to walk, run, jog, ski, or travel into the outdoors to energetically connect with the beauty, glory and majesty of the breeze, sights and sounds that envelope you.

Sketching/Drawing:
Create a drawing which represents your link with the planet, and notice any symbols that appear.

Journal:
Write messages from each planet element – Water, Wind, Earth and Fire – to your soul. Create a word-mapping page. In the center of the page, write the word that represents who or what you wish to dialogue with, circle it and then draw a line from the main circle and write the word that comes to you. Circle it and continue on in this pattern until you feel drawn to begin writing in a narrative format.

Receptivity:

Become quiet with the intention of hearing from within what you need to know in order to become more in tune with Planet Whispers. Through this time of receiving, your heart, mind and soul will be filled more fully with your radiant truth, light and wisdom.

Gratitude:

Give thanks and praise daily for all that you have through an Attitude of Gratitude Journal. Write down a list of five things you are thankful for each day. Let the universal planet know that you appreciate all the gifts and blessings that you receive, moment by moment. Conscious acknowledgement is powerful.

Fellow Soul and Terrestrial Traveler, I trust that if you haven't yet heard your Planet Whispers, you will – as you move, change and flow with your life experiences, opening your heart, mind and soul more fully to bridge the gap between your tangible and intangible worlds. The way you are meant to relate to these whispers will be revealed to you as you step forward, remembering to listen with your ego safely in your back pocket. Let your soul soar and receive the beauty, the glory, and the majesty of Planet Whispers!

∽

JENNY PALMER
Adelaide, South Australia

JENNY HAS TAUGHT IN educational settings for 34 years, working with children of all ages. She currently teaches art to 13–17 year olds. For more than two decades, Jenny has studied culture, religion, traditional and alternative modalities with numerous certifications, and has worked alongside indigenous teachers, building an extensive knowledge base and practice. Jenny is an ordained minister with the Universal Life Church of California and on the Inner Planes in the Brotherhood of Melchizedek, attained through extensive study with Dr. Joshua Stone. She is also a Usui Reiki master/teacher of 16 years and offers training to all levels.

As an author, Jenny has contributed to various educational resource publications, including Lee Carroll and Jan Tober's book *Indigo Children*, and articles such as *Teaching Indigo Children* for the Canadian magazine, *Imprint*. Jenny is writing a book on her journey as a multiple walk-in.

In 2004, Jenny began making vibrational essences in conjunction with Spirit, which now includes 15 different ranges with over 600 bottles. More recently, she became certified in Gateway Dreaming™ and offers dream coaching and classes. Jenny's skills include reading the Akashic Records and seeing Spirit Guides and Animals. Her drawings and mandalas have travelled around the globe, from Australia and New Zealand, the UK and USA to Iceland. She creates artworks for both individuals and businesses. Jenny is studying Transpersonal Art Therapy and hopes to soon have her own studio where all of her gifts and teachings can be based.

Contact www.bluelotuscreations.com.au

Through the Veil

JENNY PALMER

*Planet whispers can happen anywhere, in any landscape,
at any time, to anyone, whether one travels or not.*

The story I am about to share occurred in two interconnected locations. The first is a small ex-railway-siding town called Woods Point, 12 kilometers south of the township of Murray Bridge in South Australia, on my own property. The second location is an Adelaide Hills campsite, about 50 kilometers away. What connected these sites was a message that was brought to me by the spirit of the land. Though extreme, the experiences I describe, like all shamanic experiences, have brought positive transformation with them. I hope my story shines a light for others along the way.

The planet can whisper to you anywhere. 'Power spots' or sacred sites, to which thousands of people make their pilgrimage, are not the only places in which connections can be made between self and Spirit. In my own backyard, I twice experienced something truly mystical and magical. And again Spirit contacted me on a school camp. The possibilities are limitless regarding where connections to Spirit can be made. This was a lesson for me in being open to connecting with Spirit anytime, anywhere.

Up until my move to Woods Point I had pursued spiritual learning, taking courses and workshops in numerous modalities. I was a Reiki practitioner and had made the choice to become a Master/Teacher. Previously, I had studied with a Native American, focusing on connecting soul and Earth. So I wasn't new to Spirit, though perhaps not fully open to receiving messages from the trees, the birds, the sky and the very air I breathed.

The timing between the events I describe was no more than a few weeks apart. And the details of what occurred are as vivid as if they had happened today. I witnessed and experienced something extraordinary, without going anywhere and without doing anything special, with no preparation, no meditation, ritual or ceremony. Allow me to retrace a little…

At the beginning of 1995 I purchased 7 acres of land for my pony stud, to which I relocated my two stallions, several mares and youngsters along with my Quarter Horse, from my property on the outskirts of Murray Bridge, 16 kilometers away.

My new home was surrounded by irrigated flood plains on which dairy cattle grazed and lucerne crops bloomed with purple flowers. It was bordered on one side by natural scrub which gave me a sense of seclusion. Sheets of limestone around my buildings showed evidence of fossilized river creatures and shells, on and just below the topsoil of sand, suggesting that the primary water source, the Murray River, once lay over this ancient land.

I moved there alone, without extended family, adults and children, sharing intimately in each others' daily lives. It was a chance for me, for the first time in the 36 years of my existence, to live my life just for me.

The area, once open and free in the distant past, had been replaced with crops and cattle, buildings and a railway, a hub of industry in pioneering times. Now only a few scattered farm houses dot the landscape. It was as if the land and her early people had been forgotten, masked behind the veil of civilization. Who knew what had come before?

In the furthest corner of my property, the northeast, I had a chicken coop where the young roosters would attack me when I entered to collect the eggs from the hens. In the same area was a section I had corded off with a single strand of electric wire, for a pony to graze in to control the grass. Both the pony and the horse I tried locating there would either jump out or crash through the electric wire. These animals were used to being surrounded by electric fences. But there was something there that was making them skittish, no matter the pain or the loss of feed it cost them by leaving this lush area.

Late one summer night, around 10pm it began. The moon was full. An unwelcome chill rippled through me as I sat on my couch with Holly, my collie, at my feet and Egypt, my cat, beside me. In that moment everything changed. My eyes became hazy and it was a challenge to see clearly. I was drifting back through the veil of time, to a time before man, as we know him to look today, walked this place called Earth.

As the images began to enter my living room, the couch I was sitting on disappeared. The windows and curtains were gone, the floor turning to grass. And there in front of me in the darkness of night was a roaring fire, with figures floating in the air, feet not touching the ground. The fire mesmerized them with its licking and leaping flames, coaxing the dancers closer and closer to its source. They were transformed in a frenzy of singing, chanting and whirling.

As this scene continued, I saw a sacrifice and blood. A body fell limply to the ground yet was still alive. Then the next figure I saw was fighting against restraining hands, struggling to get free. In the far corner, by the chicken coop (which wasn't there now) bodies were being buried. Yet they were trying to free themselves. I realized they were live sacrifices! The ground had since wept with the memories of these deaths. The anger of the souls, buried alive, to die, were what the roosters and ponies were responding to in fear.

It was as if there was a crossover between both times – I was in their time and they were in mine. Feeling like a thief, stealing a glance at what was only for the Holy men of the tribe to see; terror peaked and flooded my body with adrenalin. One of them turned towards me, looking through me, into me. I could feel his eyes and his mind probing deeply into my very bones, my very core. My breath stopped, poised for his response – but there was none, verbally or physically. He made no move toward me, yet I felt him touching me, his essence penetrating and intermingling with mine.

With a flash, as fast it came, I was back, sitting on my couch in the living room, with its windows, my pets, as if nothing had happened. Somewhat disoriented and distressed, I phoned an intuitive friend asking for her advice or interpretation of what had just occurred. She referred me to a gentleman with some knowledge of ritual, with whom I had once had a spiritual reading.

I was shocked when he advised that I make a blood sacrifice, by killing one of the hens or roosters to offer its blood. Since I was unable to bring myself to do this, he suggested that I prick my finger deep enough to draw blood. Following his suggestion, it took what seemed like forever to apply adequate pressure to a bloodless finger to encourage enough blood to surface so that I might prick it. I knew I had to do this alone, for me. A single drop of blood appeared on my finger, yet I had pushed the needle in quite deeply. I squeezed, yet no more blood would come. I then applied this single drying drop to the soil of the land where I sat. It burned like nothing else I had ever experienced. It was as if my finger had been held over a burning ember or a hotplate and allowed to burn. Though the pain was intense, I held my finger to the soil until it subsided.

The next part of his instruction was to take moon water that I was to make this very night and sprinkle this over the entire area, from inside the living room, to around the fire area and out into the furthest corner of the property, including the chicken coop. This was to cleanse and release any of the trapped souls. I did this in such a daze; I don't remember the words I spoke during this process.

It seemed to me that I was witnessing life when it was based upon the Earth and her worship, coupled with a higher Being, personified as a god or gods, for whom sacrifices were carried out, to appease the needs of the god, to sustain the eternal flame. These fire ceremonies and rituals were a testament to a people's cultural belief in something which was greater than themselves, and a force, or energy source, beyond my comprehension.

My shifted state of consciousness left me in fear of traveling across time and space, seemingly without any semblance of control or knowledge of what to do, without any choice about whether to accept it or shut it off. I was inexperienced in this, and in the power of the moment, I had not yet realized the subtleties of the message being conveyed to me in this vision.

The second experience came on a day prior to taking a group of children on a school camp, a short time after the first vision of the fire ceremony. The excursion involved taking 11 year olds from three classes to a bush site in a small Hills community with two other male teachers. I awoke on that Sunday morning prior to the camping trip, unable to walk properly. I was suffering acute pain in my pelvis, and when I tried to walk, my feet could only shuffle, barely passing each other. Just getting dressed was a challenge. The impending thought of trying to sleep in a sleeping bag raised an anxiety within me that consumed me.

Night had fallen and I couldn't move. I rang a healer friend who was like a mother to me, who lived on the other side of Murray Bridge. Whilst I spoke to her, I screamed with a sharp shooting pain in my abdomen. Being alone experiencing this level of pain was not an option. I had to seek help to ease both my fear and the pain. As she couldn't drive, I somehow drove the 30 kilometers to her house. As I knelt to get up onto her massage table, I was struck with a pain that ripped through my belly as if I was being sliced open. It was as though a radiating fire was burning my insides. It knocked the breath out of me. All I could do was kneel on all fours whilst she held me, until the pain subsided.

My friend said she smelled cloves and embalming fluids while I was experiencing the sensation of being cut open. The point was that I was wide awake and fully conscious as this was occurring. We both realized that what I was witnessing and feeling was the experience of being mummified in a past life, while still alive. In a vision, I had been sent to retrieve information from the gods. When, after the usual three days, they opened the sarcophagus, and my spirit had not returned and I appeared dead, the embalming process had begun.

The following day I went to the camp, but could barely walk. Therefore I was left in charge of the campfire while the other teachers took the children on a hike. A half hour later when they all returned, the fire which had been a huge bonfire built taller than me and roaring with energy and vitality, was but a few embers, despite my feeding it fuel continuously.

Returning home after the camp, I rang the man who had helped me previously with the fire ceremony vision. He received information that I was to come to peace with fire. And this meant completion of an initiation begun long ago. I was to find a basement or cellar, a place where I could be in absolute darkness and remain there for a minimum of three hours, before returning to the surface, at ground level. Panic welled as my greatest fear was exposed – fear of the dark, of being trapped alive in a place from which I couldn't escape without help. Thus he suggested an alternative – staying in a floatation tank for three cubed (equaling twenty-seven) minutes, after which time my name could then be called out and I would be invited back.

I completed the floatation tank exercise, with some fear. When I felt overwhelmed inside the tank, I flicked on the light inside to see where I was. The space was not large enough for my body to turn around, and yet I was convinced that I had been spinning and turning in a whirlpool.

The facilitator called my name, via microphone, and invited me back into this realm, in this time and in this place. This brought back memories of an earlier sweat lodge experience where I couldn't stay inside the lodge for the final round and the Comanche facilitator had me move outside to eat something sweet. He was unable to ascertain the reason for this. It happened time and again. The fire and the heat made it impossible for me to remain inside the sweat lodge. My pulses became visible in the veins of my neck and face, looking so close to rupture he thought I'd self-combust. It was then that he received his own vision, to 'open' my ceremonial pipe. He asked me after its opening, "Just who are you?"

The element of heat connected to the campfire (too little or too much), coupled with the Beings involved with the fire ceremony vision, as well as the sarcophagus event, all had a common theme – Fire.

I thought I had found a connection. I was evidently finding it a challenge to keep my internal/eternal flame burning. My life force seemed to be dying.

Over the past several years before this, I had experienced several of the chronic fatigue viruses and I had little energy to do anything, even to carry water and feed to the ponies. Joy seemed to slip through my fingers. I was alone, isolated from friends and family by distance. It was as if I'd been retreating further and further away from everyone and everything.

I am what some may call a 'multiple walk-in' and at this point, what I called the 'phoenix energy' was begin-

> ### Courage
>
> *Each new day brings opportunities to learn and grow.*
>
> *Before a baby bird emerges from an egg, it must first break through a shell. The beginning of a quest may involve obstacles, though help is always available on request. By moving bravely forward, clarity emerges, allowing us to connect with who we truly are.*

ning to merge with me, as dragon energy which had been in full throttle was now stepping down. My humanness was the bridge between the guardian and protector energies of the dragon, and the transformation and re-birthing energies of the phoenix. More references to fire. I was given the impression this was all connected with my ability to transmute and completely rebirth myself, like the phoenix born out of the ashes. I have since honored this with tattoos of both the dragon and the phoenix. Along with the tattoos of my other energies, before and after these, my body now speaks my story.

The Fire Element is the spirit-dominated element. In addition to witnessing the vision of the fire ceremony in my living room, and being unable to keep the bonfire burning, there had been two fires in my kitchen. I also had difficulties getting a match to strike, and I couldn't light the then three year old, ceremonial pipe.

Did I truly and fully understand the significance of these planetary whispers to me? Until recently, I had not fully considered the true messages of these experiences in 1995 – what they were bringing to me, and how this would change my world.

I now see more, as the layers unravel and the petals unfold, as the lotus energy now reigns within me, out of the darkness and into the light. These experiences took me to a place that allowed me to reconnect with self and make decisions for myself, instead of doing what others expected of me.

I have realized, only now, the roles the three individuals involved with those experiences have played in this life, my life, here and now. The first lady played the past life role of the ceremonial leader for the sacrifices and also the embalmer. The man was my teacher who was unable to bring me, the initiate, back after I had left the body in the sarcophagus to commune with the gods. His involvement in these events in this current time, was his returning to reconcile what he had been unable to do, in a time long past. And the mother-like lady was my healer when I had returned from Spirit and awoke in the sarcophagus, who healed me, all those millennia ago.

Prior to this, I thought I was a sponge for this universal knowledge. Now I knew there was a world that existed out there, untouched, unexplored and not yet experienced. I wanted to taste every bit of it. My pursuit of spiritual knowledge and who I am increased exponentially after this.

Looking back at the moment I was physically sitting on the couch, both in this world and also standing in another, by the circle, I knew. I knew that there was no difference between one space and another. Both were happening simultaneously, as if time was not as we know it. It was a profound reminder that time, space and dimension are one, enfolding over and in on itself.

I made the connection between the ceremonial fire and sacrifices – being buried alive and left to die, and the death in the sarcophagus. Only now is it obvious that my life was being buried. The very essence of who I am was dying, yet now to be ignited and reclaimed. Reborn.

My life was changing. A door had been opened through fire, the dark being shown its light. As I accepted what had occurred, even if I didn't fully understand it, I stepped into a realm of being, unimpeded by my world. Boundaries and limitations merged into one and were lifted as I realized there was so much more to the Cosmos and my self. It aided me in transforming my life, changing my focus, shifting me in new directions. Though I didn't quite know what that was at the time.

The original dream to have a pony stud in the country was not actually mine. I had fallen in with family choices and making decisions based on their approval. The peaceful life alone, close to nature, was shifting, changing. My physical body was slowing down. My skin had become noticeably grey and somewhat transparent.

I then began making choices that primarily were for me, and me alone. And that meant the exclusion of the pony stud dream. Thus I sold everything, the ponies and the house and returned to the city, allowing myself time to bridge the changes and find my own path and direction. In spite of this, I realize that those eighteen years living on a pony stud had helped to keep me grounded to the earth.

My life and new views on all things began to make changes in me that were permanent. I looked at these events without terror and disbelief. Nothing from this time forward could surprise me or shock me. It was another turning point for me, and I knew I'd never be the same. My own channeling increased with the inclusion of nature, the elements and the animals. The pursuit to know more about myself, my other lives (not only on Earth) and how they impacted on who I was now, in this moment, and why I saw what I did, grew phenomenally. It brought me to a place of joy in getting to know the true me.

After these events, I came to connect with a female Maori elder, who would say to me, "Listen to the trees Eaglehawk, (as she called me) to the wind and to the birds. Can you not hear what they are saying to you? Feel the earth rumble as you speak to me over distance and know that your energy is one with the earth." In her presence, during a circle, I had visions passing before me in front of fire. I witnessed many things around my being 'born,' repeatedly within this body. She allowed me and encouraged me to stay in this space, simply smiling when it was complete.

My life has been and is a journey of integration of that which is spiritual with that which is Earth living. Every breath I take, I live as Spirit having a human experience.

The last energy to enter my body, in 2002, was born in Sagittarius-fire, and is known as Blue Lotus. Symbolic in itself, it continues with the theme of my life – perpetual change and growth, from the dark depths of my very core, to blossom in the light and back again, a cycle of the creation of self. And this too, is tattooed with the same honor I have given each of my energies, a reminder of my journey.

Planet whispers can happen anywhere, in any landscape, at any time, to anyone, whether one travels or not. The whispers are forever present, whether in the silence and stillness, or amidst chaos. When heard, they bring transformation and set in motion the answers to the perpetual question "Who am I and why am I here?" The focus of being human is seeing more of self, understanding more of self and becoming more of self.

Tuning In
How does one tune into these energies? Can they affect consciousness? Can they produce transformations in one's identity, or concept of self? Most certainly!

Begin by creating a sacred space within self. This will be wherever self is. It is where the reality, the truth unveils itself. It can be anywhere. Expectations only limit that which may come. Be open and unwavering to that which soul chooses to bring forth, by whatever means. Allow what comes before you to be seen, heard or felt. Information may come instantaneously or it may filter in over weeks, months and even years, as my 'fire' experiences have done.

I hear many say they are frustrated by cryptic messages, asking why can't it be straight-forward, to the point? They want it *now*. Getting all the information at once, then releasing and changing instantly is unlikely. Patterns of belief take time to create and thus to transform. Fears and resistance can be brought into the open to be acknowledged and released.

Face the fears that surface within, and then check your feelings on all levels – physical, emotional, intellectual, spiritual, self, etheric and auric. Avoid backing away, as this is resistance and serves only to hinder self. Resisting the resistance can bring more problems, struggle and pain. The core self chooses the release or it would not surface and show itself.

Light a candle or incense to connect with fire and to bring a focus point. My Comanche teacher taught me 20 years ago, to use the flame and the incense to offer blessing and the light to Father Sky, Mother Earth, all the Directions and all the Elements. I say this as I raise my hand above, then below, and circle for the last two, before circling the incense stick around my body, thus connecting me with All That Is, as well. I continue doing this to this day.

Now, physically connect with the temple that is the body – feel it, hear it, every muscle, every blood cell, every bone, every organ, every vessel and tissue, and every subatomic particle.

Emotionally allow the sensations to flood through the body, giving expression to the feelings and observe.

Intellectually let the chatter reveal itself and then subside, to choose its own focus, if there is one.

Spiritually connect with that which is beyond self, to soul. This could be with mantra, meditation and affirmation.

Integrate the self (the physical, emotional, intellectual and spiritual as one) by feeling the core that is self. Breathe into this center.

The etheric (the physical body double) is the energetic shield and bridge through which all prior levels are transmuted. Sense and witness this field, that of self.

Auricly, (the spiritual double) know that everything is also nothing, and in stillness there is also movement, and that all this exists at once.

There is no other place in this solar system where a being can go to experience all seven of these levels in the one lifetime, other than Earth, making this planet a truly mystical and magical place to be. The planet teaches and shows the way.

Feel her heartbeat and her breath as if it is your body's own heartbeat and breath. Open your heart to that which the soul is bringing. Be still in the silence – relax, breathe, and let self touch self/soul. Sink into that place within that is balanced and fearless. Feel…

The doorway to self is within self! Believe that connection is possible and probable and it will be so. Then one moves between dimensions consciously, deliberately. One taps into all of that which is self. Refrain from looking for the grand and remain open to the small and subtle whispers. For in every whisper is a universe of information about self.

Teacher

*I give thanks for all I learn
and experience.*

*As we work to improve ourselves,
attaining valuable life knowledge
along the way, we birth the teacher
within. The lessons learned through
purifying ourselves and honing our
skills lead naturally to passing on the
wisdom gained to others.*

KAREN JARLDANE
Boulder, Colorado, USA

KAREN HAS BEEN DRAWN to stones, sacred sites and the mysteries of spirit all her life. Her own home pushed her into a path of self-discovery, opening her eyes to the magic of working consciously with the earth to create harmony in homes and the land. Learning to use the natural rhythms and patterns of the sun to create wonderful structures such as stone circles and labyrinths has been very exciting and fulfilling for her. Karen is dedicated to bringing back this lost knowledge and creating more harmony for all by sharing her wisdom through teaching at Boulder Centre for Master Builders.

Karen studied with Denise Linn and is an Interior Alignment® Practitioner. She has also been involved with ongoing studies with French Master Dominique Susani in the Ancient Art of Stones, dowsing, natural geometry and earth energies since 2002. Karen is passionate about creating meditation places, labyrinths, stone circles and more, using natural geometry. She also loves traveling around the world diving into the mysteries of sacred sites with the help of dowsing and sensing with her body the energies in each place.

Karen invites you to check out her website to learn more about the Art of the Master Builders and to see the current class schedule, at www.boulder masterbuilders.com.

Whispers from My Home

KAREN JARLDANE

*To build a powerful machine such as a stone circle,
it is best to blend the energies of heaven and earth.*

*I*t was all my home's fault! It led me on a journey of discovery that turned out to be my life's path, and helped me deepen my relationship with Mother Earth. Before having kids, I was an Air Force Reserve Pilot, flying around the world dropping off troops and cargo. I also flew for Pan Am, based in Germany and experienced the Berlin Wall falling firsthand. I truly enjoyed exploring different lands and cultures, so it was surprising to me that it was in my own backyard that I heard the whisper, not in some far flung reaches of the world. Ok, I admit, it was more like a shout…

The story began with my husband shopping for a home in Boulder, Colorado, while I stayed in California taking care of a newborn and an eighteen-month-old child. He only had a few hours to find a suitable house and he succeeded. His vision was simple: we needed a home where our children had enough room to grow, play and be safe.

My first sight of our new Coloradoan home was driving up to it after the long journey from California. The house looked wonderful; it was brand new, big, with a huge yard on a cul-de-sac. As far as my husband was concerned, it was perfect. It was for me too until I realized how close we lived to high voltage power lines. They were next to our backyard fence and to make matters worse, a few blocks away stood a power substation. I knew it was not good for our health to live so close to them.

During the process of becoming a mother, I tuned into my intuition on a whole new level. With the protective instincts of a mother for her young, I knew I had to make our home better. It felt buzzy, ungrounded, and my husband was more edgy, sometimes explosive. He has a natural ability to sense different energies (without realizing it) and was obviously effected by the power lines. I wanted to fix the problem and bring harmony back to our lives, so I started researching how to shift and balance the electrical nature of our home.

First I explored how Feng Shui could help and had our home professionally Feng Shui'd. We moved furniture around until the house felt better to me. I found this so interesting that I took further classes in Feng Shui. Our home flowed better but there was still something to be worked on. I dove in deeper and became certified as an Interior Alignment® Practitioner by Denise Linn.

Learning from Denise about different modalities to help homes feel better was fascinating and opened my mind to a myriad of possibilities. I learned about Space Clearing from her and removed the negative energy from our home. Then I took a class about devas, nature spirits and angels and how they can help heal. There is a whole unseen world out there, willing to help us clean up our mess with Mother Earth. Humans have not worked with nature as a partner in a long time. Working with the nature spirits taught me about how to engage with them and the earth co-creatively as a partner. I realized there is much to 'clean up' physically and energetically.

Each of these techniques helped shift the energy of my home and taught me how to deepen my relationship with the earth and its helpers; but it wasn't enough. My house was still buzzy and felt good for a time, then reverted back to the way it was. I needed to go deeper, but didn't know how.

Then out of blue it came, an email that changed my life. 'Druid Geomancy' read the subject line. I was intrigued. There was a class in Santa Fe taught by a French druid. He was teaching dowsing, geomancy and something about big stones. The class sounded so interesting that I decided to go on a road trip to Santa Fe and take the weekend course.

The Path

*The light of my soul
illuminates my path.*

*The goal is important, yet there is joy
in noticing how far we have come. By
looking back at our beginnings, we
see the blessings of the path we have
chosen. Progress comes when every
stepping stone we create benefits
others. All paths return to the
sanctuary of the heart,
our true soul home.*

Dominique Susani it turns out, looks like a Druid. He has a wonderful sense of humor, is short, has his long grey hair braided down his back, speaks only French and Spanish, and teaches things I'd never heard about before. Here was somebody who knew how to harmonize a home on a deep level and didn't just talk about it; we were outside dowsing and tuning our bodies to feel the sensations of the earth. I was hooked.

Dowsing can be difficult and sometimes confusing work. After a while, your body is done sensing and you can't feel anything else. Many of the energies under the earth are noxious to us and it is best not to sleep over them. Learning how electrical energy can contaminate water or fault lines that naturally flow around our earth and under our houses was a big *aha!* moment for me and the problems with my home. I needed to learn how to neutralize this electrical energy.

It is interesting to look back and see how events orchestrate themselves around what you most need to learn. My home was whispering to me... fix me!!! Dominique ended up being the perfect teacher for my home. During that weekend workshop I ended up asking him to come to Boulder to teach. I hungered to learn more from him and knew I had to make it happen.

In the years that followed, Dominique flew to Boulder once a year to teach, and I learned amazing things each time; from geomancy and dowsing, to harmonizing homes by placing stones around them. He is a unique teacher. You learn by feeling the energies of the earth in your body and from there, a profound knowing, deep within, is felt when harmony is created.

We spent part of the classes drawing mandalas that are actual patterns of the sun's path throughout the year, highlighting the summer and winter solstice sunrises and sunsets. Each spot on earth has different characteristics because the angle of the sun is different, depending on how north or south of the equator you live. The next part of the classes were then spent outside drawing the same patterns on the ground, and feeling the energy of the natural geometry that arises from the earth when you put weight on these key points.

Our ancestors used these same mandalas created by the sun's path throughout the year to build their homes, their sacred sites, and more. All cultures around the world have used the sun's pattern as a basis for their sacred site planning. They built their temples and churches using different characteristics of the same pattern, according to their cultural values. For an Art History major like me, this was the missing link!

There was another language being spoken at these places of power. Besides being architecturally marvelous, many of these sights were consciously built using the energies of the earth and the cosmos. They are powerful healing places because of this, and I now understood why people are attracted to these sacred sites. Sadly though, the knowledge of how to build our homes, communities, and sacred places in alignment with the sun was lost during the time when science began taking over our perceptions, and we were taught to believe only what we see, not what we feel.

How wonderful it would be if we could take this ancient wisdom that is being revived with Dominique's work and use it to build places that are harmonized from the very beginning! How much happier we could be, living in a place that supports us, rather than working against us... like my home.

As I gained experience and learned new techniques from Dominique each year, I put my knowledge to the test on my home. I dowsed my house, noting where the water lines and faults lines were. I moved beds away from these lines. This helped and we slept better now our beds were off these underground energies.

Next, I installed stone patterns called 'solsticial quadrilaterals' around our home for each person's birthplace. What you do is put four big stones in each corner of the rectangle of the sun's pattern. I had several different rock rectangles because we were all born in different cities! After the stones were placed, it felt calmer and the buzzy feeling was somewhat dissipated.

Next time Dominique visited he said, "Tch, tch, tch, bigger is better with stones!" Since I live so close to the high power lines, more weight from larger stones would help 'push down' the energies of the faults and water, neutralizing them more efficiently. Even though my home felt healthier, there was still more work to be done.

Then, we learned about one-point harmonizations. This is when you use one stone to harmonize the whole place. It is trickier to find the right spot. You need to use your senses more. But when you find the right point and align the stone properly, your body clearly tells you this is it!

When a stone is placed well, you can feel the alignment in your body's central channel. In other words, you can feel the energy from the earth connect with the cosmos and you are the pipeline for the energy exchange between the two! You feel completely open to the heavens and are connected to the earth, feeling the exchange of energies between them. It feels good. If the alignment between the two is not right, you will feel it in your body as nausea, or of a place of being stuck. The flow between heaven and earth has stopped.

For the one-point harmonization on my home, I enlisted the help of my consultant friends to find the correct position for my stone. When the right place was found and we placed the stone, it felt good. A feeling of calm settled over us unlike any other time. I was excited by this change because it felt bigger than anything else I had done to the house.

Shortly after placing the stone, something happened with one of my boys that would usually send my husband through the roof. Amazingly, he was calmer and more centered when dealing with the problem. My husband is a good barometer for me of what is going on with the energy of our home. If he was off, then something still needed to be done with our home. This time there was a big shift in his reaction in a good way. After consulting Dominique about the one-point harmonization and my husband's reaction, he said I was done, and not to do anything else to my home! I was very happy to finally finish this healing work. It took years of learning and trying different techniques, but I finally got it right!

As my wisdom matured in working with the energies of heaven and earth to harmonize homes, my abilities to draw the mandalas of the sun's patterns developed. I had a better understanding of how the different elements come together when a harmonized place is built. The Master Builders of old would have spent years designing important sites such as Stonehenge, New Grange, or Romanesque churches. They would incorporate into their designs the sun and moon's alignments, the elements of water, fire, air, ether, spirit, and the blend of masculine and feminine energies. Learning about this truly excited me!

I loved the idea of creating a home, meditation place, stone circle or labyrinth using a mixture of these elements, and was eager to learn how to do this. Thus we decided to create a workshop to build a cromlech; a stone circle similar to Stonehenge, but using much smaller stones!

In prior classes I only needed to find a place to hold the workshop, but this time it was different. When Dominique sent me an email telling me I needed to find 'a blind spring in a free place,' I was apprehensive about my abilities to find just the right spot for our cromlech. It was a test of my abilities on an unspoken level.

To build a powerful machine such as a stone circle, it is best to blend the energies of heaven and earth. Through dowsing, we learn how to find the energies of the earth, such as water veins, faults and blind springs. In ancient times, Master Builders spent time searching for specific underground energies to give certain healing qualities to their churches, stone circles or labyrinths. Many churches were built on very specific places to take advantage of either the healing properties of water or the fire energy of faults.

For the 'heaven' part of the equation, our drawings of the mandalas come into play. To start, we use the pattern formed by the sun's path throughout the year to build our cromlech. Solstice sunrises and sunsets were important to ancient people and were observed and marked on the earth throughout the year. When this is done, the shape of a rectangle is formed on the ground. This is the beginning pattern we use in drawing our mandalas called the "Solsticial Quadrilateral."

The center of our cromlech needed to be an underground 'blind spring' rising towards the surface of the earth, but which doesn't reach daylight due to something blocking its ascent. It then branches out under the ground in many directions like spokes on a wheel. I was nervous about my abilities for finding a suitable energetic center point from which to build our cromlech, since finding a spot that matched these specifications, though difficult, would give much better energetic qualities to our stone circle.

My dear friend Cat who has taken many of Dominique's classes helped me on this quest. We searched for days for the right place. It needed to be free of electrical contamination from the ground. Nothing in town would work because of this. It needed to be in a place where people could enjoy it freely, thus eliminating someone's private property. We couldn't have a big boulder or tree in the middle of our stone circle either.

You find a blind spring by dowsing and using the sensibilities of your body to feel the quality of the water. As the weeks passed in our search for the perfect spot, we finally found a clearing that looked like it might work. It was just a feeling we both had as we looked at this certain place. So we explored the energy further by dowsing for water, and it turned out to be a blind spring! Then we felt the quality of the water. To do this, you stand over the point you have chosen, close your eyes and sense the water with your body. Ours felt good and free from electrical or other contamination. If you feel nauseous, you need to find another spot. Hopefully we had found a good spot, since the energetic qualities of this center point would set the tone for our cromlech. Now we were ready for our teacher and the stone-circle-making class to begin.

We spent the first day of the class drawing the mandala of the stone circle. Dominique always creates fresh designs so no two are the same. For this cromlech, we worked with the energy of the solstices. We drew the cromlech using the sun circle. For Boulder, this is strong energy because it is close to one of the fire circles in the mandala, which relates to a cosmic, spirit type energy. It is one of the unique characteristics of Boulder. When I first moved here, it took me a few years to get used to this energy. For me, the Flatiron Mountains seemed to shoot the energy high into the heavens. It felt cosmic and more masculine in flavor than my childhood state of California, which had the ocean and felt more feminine and embracing.

So it made sense to me that Boulder's characteristics when drawing the mandala were solar-masculine, with a connection to spirit. When you draw mandalas the way Dominique teaches, you are connecting both sides of your brain. At first it can be hard to use a compass to make perfect circles, and rulers to draw perfect squares. It is easy to feel out of your depth, but with practice, the drawings become more precise and you can feel with your body the energy that flows from a good mandala.

The next day, we reviewed the drawing, gathered up our materials, magnetic compasses to site true north, bamboo sticks to mark points, measuring tapes to make sure our distances were correct, and hiked to the spot we had selected. My test of being a good apprentice was at hand. Did I pick out a good spot or not? Dominique stood on our chosen point, feeling the energy of the earth beneath him and smiled at Cat and me. "It's a good one," he said. We excitedly jumped up and down with happiness. For me, this was an initiation into the next step of my training with him.

Dominique teaches in an old European style of Master and Apprentice. What he teaches cannot be learned in a quick weekend course. It takes time and experience working with the material, to learn more and graduate to the next level. You can't learn more than what you can take in and process. The American culture of "I want it now" style of teaching often clashes with what Dominique has to offer.

In the next part of the class, using the blind spring as our center, we drew our mandala on the ground, orienting it to the four directions and true north. It is important to use directions corrected for true north. This is how the ancient people built their sacred sites, since magnetic north did not line up with the sun's patterns. Before creating our circle, we first drew the solsticial quadrilateral or rectangle on the ground. This would connect our stone circle to the heavens or cosmos. From this point, we added more measurements and points until we had marked all the spots for the stone placements. We each found several different stones to set in our marked points.

An important part of the equation is orienting the stones properly. Stones have an earth side and a cosmic side that you need to feel with your sensibilities. You can use your hand to feel the warmth of the cosmos side or the coolness of the earth side. Stones also have a point on them that is aligned to magnetic north that needs to be aligned on the ground with the earth's magnetic north. To make positioning the stone even harder, it needs to be adjusted so that you feel your central channel open and flowing between the balance of the earth and heaven's energies. It can be very frustrating at times. Your stone can be upside down and you don't realize it, or it doesn't have a good vertical axis to work with, or it just feels bad. Dominique was quite busy helping us align our stones just right.

After the last stone was placed in the circle, we got to experience the fun part of all our hard work! One person would stand in the center and feel the quality of the energy of the stone circle, while the others walked around the cromlech clockwise, activating and opening the energy of the circle. Once momentum from our circling started, the person in the middle was able to feel it.

The first time I stood there, I could feel the energy that we were generating, spreading outwards in waves. It was quite strong and Dominique decided to tweak it a bit. He told Cat and me to go find one more stone for the center. After placing and aligning it properly, instead of the energy flowing outwards, now it went straight up to the heavens! Wow, it was powerful. The stone circle created from the energy of the sun here in Boulder was strong and Dominique was well pleased with what we accomplished.

I knew there was much more for me to learn, however I was happy with the wisdom I had gained. My home, which seemed bad at first, sent me on a journey of discovery. I learned many healing techniques for my home and the earth. I have new allies to work with co-creatively. I found an amazing teacher as well a totally different career and life path.

Before having kids and settling down, I was a pilot flying around the world. Now I am working with stones, creating harmony for people and their homes. I'm sensing earth energies, drawing amazing mandalas, and building powerful healing machines for people to raise their vibrations and cleanse their energy. Certainly there is much more for me to learn, but looking back through the years with my home whispering to me, I am grateful for the path it sent me on.

Marking the Solstices

After studying with Dominique for years and learning about the sun's travel throughout the year, I was startled to realize I hadn't actually paid much attention to it. My big moment of "Oh this is what he is talking about" happened after driving my boys to a bus stop each morning for months.

We always enjoyed watching the sunrise and the colors that join the sun as it rises. Then it hit me: hey the sun used to rise over by that tree a few months ago and now it is coming up over here by this barn!

You can notice the same thing with either the sunrise each morning or the sunset if it is easier to track. Just become aware of the position of the sun each morning or evening as it rises or sets, and you will begin to see the journey it makes throughout the year. It is fun to become more aware of the natural rhythms of the sun, as it begins to tune your body to the language of the Master Builders.

Next, we will explore a much more involved exercise to become more aware of the sun's travel throughout the year. You will specifically mark the position of the solstices in your area.

Solstice actually means 'sun stand still.' The solstices mark the point where the sun's furthest northern or southern travel reverses. This was important to our ancestors and they had different ways of marking this occasion and using it in their buildings. It is well known that many megalithic structures showcase the sunrise or sunset for the solstices.

Stonehenge is one of the most popular sites where people gather each year to witness the rise of the sun in alignment with well-placed stones. Our ancient ancestors could feel how the alignment of buildings and other structures with the sun's patterns actually benefited them and their communities. Feeling the effects of these alignments is something we have lost as we've became more modernized.

It is easy for you to mark these solstice points for yourself. All it takes is some patience and a sunny day to mark your points. Doing this the old fashion way takes time though, and you may be able to understand why it took years for the Master Builders to align their structures properly. It takes one year to mark the summer and winter solstice sunrise and sunset positions.

To begin with, you will need a place where you can observe the sunrises and sunsets, hopefully unobstructed by homes, mountains etc. Next you will need a pole to mark your center. This pole or stick should be around one meter or three feet tall. You can identify the correct day by consulting your calendar or looking it up online. Then, for a couple of days before and after the winter or summer solstice, you can mark with a bamboo stick where the sun rises if you are standing and seeing the sun from your center pole.

In other words, you and your pole are the center. You face east and look towards the sunrise and mark a point along this angle in relation to the center pole. (You and the sunrise form a line, so mark your point along this line). In the evening, you will be facing the opposite direction (west) and will do the same thing. Stand directly behind your center pole, facing in the direction of the setting sun. The instant the sun disappears beneath the horizon, site this angle and mark it with another bamboo pole.

It is best to have these two measurements the same distance from the center pole, because after you measure the winter solstice sunrise and sunset, you will see a rectangle emerge from your measurements. This is a rudimentary solsticial quadrilateral for your place!

I hope you enjoy tuning into the energy of the sun's travel throughout the year. It is fun to become more aware of the cycles of the seasons, the moon and the sun. By doing this, I feel more connected to heaven and earth, and it is a good way to gain a deeper understanding of how our ancestors were building in alignment with the planet, long ago.

∾

SUSIE SCICLUNA
Sydney, NSW, Australia

SUSIE SCICLUNA BECAME a Theta-Healing™ practitioner in early 2010 and since then, Susie has qualified as an advanced Theta Healer. She consults from her private practice in Crows Nest, New South Wales, Australia.

Susie lives on the Lower North Shore of Sydney and while maintaining a busy working life has enjoyed raising four beautiful children. She now has four grandchildren.

Susie is passionate about helping to empower others and make a positive contribution to our world.

If you would like a consultation with Susie either in person at her practice or by phone, or to learn more about ThetaHealing™, please visit her website:

www.spiritualthetahealing.com

City of Dreams

SUSIE SCICLUNA

❧

At the top of the slope I happened to look up at a sign that had always been there.
I smiled when I read the message: "Awake Season. Are you ready?"

*S*itting in my room looking out of the window, surrounded by beautiful green trees and plants, a soft wind gently blowing the blinds to and fro... I smile. You know, one of those smiles from the inside out. I would like to share with you part of my journey, a journey that I have been on for as long as I can remember. I have been on a quest, fellow Soul Traveler, searching for so long for answers and meaning. The path has had many ups and downs. Here it is so far....

I have lived in Australia for the past thirty-four years, much of that time in Sydney's Western Suburbs, but for the past nine years on Sydney's Lower North Shore – a wonderful place to visit and an even better place to live!

Arriving at my sister's two bedroom apartment in North Sydney in the summer of 2001, to stay with her and my two nieces, I was accompanied by my little daughter aged 8. I had just left a relationship that had been very challenging, from childhood sweethearts,

to two lost souls who just couldn't work things out, whichever road we took. And speaking of roads, my fork in the road looked more like 'spaghetti junction' at that time, and my foundations were crumbling fast. My sister was kind enough to take us in so I had a temporary place to rest.

As a mother of four, I had spent of lot of time bringing my children into this beautiful city of Sydney during school holidays and weekends, exploring museums, beautiful parks and spectacular beaches. In all those travels, I had not discovered North Sydney.

It is so pretty, peaceful and historical here, all at once. Its tree lined streets, little cafes, restaurants and parks are filled with an assortment of business people, visitors and a myriad of school children. Old stone churches line old street corners, tucked away, standing the test of time, filled to capacity on Sundays. There are noodle markets on Friday evenings, with lots of different cultures offering specialty foods for hungry visitors and a band for the children and grown-ups to dance to. Saturdays bring a different type of market, with stalls brimming with crafts, clothing, jewelry, plants and home made jams and soaps, guaranteeing the discovery of a gift suitable for anyone.

As I spent my days exploring this little town, I settled into a feeling of *coming home*, unlike anything I'd experienced before. I began attending church services at St Mary's Church in Ridge Street on Sunday mornings. Father Peter was the funniest man; he joked and related everything to our everyday lives. He called the children up to act out the story he was telling, no matter how many there were, which always bought the house down… I had begun a new chapter in my life. You know, the part of the book where the story is opening up and you don't know what to expect, but you feel the anticipation and excitement? That excitement!

Magic was weaving its way back into my world. People were so friendly and helpful. The days were warm and long. I had a chance to rediscover who I was and started to think about where I was heading.

I had felt disconnected from my spiritual path, lost and very alone, although lots of family and friends surrounded me. I began to open up to my surroundings while taking long walks. Noticing the birds waking up the sleeping world at dawn with their song, I realized I too had been asleep.

As time went on, I met a lovely man through my job in real estate, a kind gentleman and a teacher to me. About six months later, I understood that he had many women in his life and I was just one more. He accompanied me to my sister's wedding in the very pretty village of McMahons Point. This quaint little village borders Sydney Harbour, taking in magnificent views of the Harbour Bridge and the Opera House. There, at the reception in our favorite Thai restaurant, I stepped outside and noticed a painting in the window of the Art Gallery next door.

The painting was of a bride and groom floating above the Harbour Bridge at night time. They were holding hands, but both had an apprehensive look on their faces. The bridge looked silver under the moon and lots of different color blues made up the sky and harbor below. The wharves poking out from the shoreline and the little ferry sailing underneath looked so magical. It precisely captured the feelings I was having about the man I was with. I knew I had to buy it!

The relationship broke up shortly afterwards, but I purchased the painting anyway. It was called the *City of Dreams*. Perfect! Later that year, I moved to an apartment in Lavender Bay, between North Sydney and McMahons Point, a wonderful place with pretty views over the Bridge and Opera House, in a small cozy building with neat gardens and lovely neighbors. As I hung my picture on the wall, I couldn't believe it! The painting was my exact view… Synchronicity was at work in my life.

About a year later, I went to the same gallery to see an exhibition of the artist's recent work. As I chatted with the beautiful Karen Atkins, I told her I had bought her painting because it captured a memory of my boyfriend and me. Karen smiled and said "That's why I painted it… to capture a memory." Karen went on to explain how she had fallen from a horse and lost her memory. As her memories began to return, she would paint them. Karen said "It's no surprise that you bought that painting. We are all connected and it's destiny." How special!

Everything in my life started to take on a magical feel. I was becoming more aware of the signs all around me. I had always made up names or words from the letters I saw on car number plates. For example, V would remind me of Vilia, my Mum's name. I would phone her and she would say "I was just thinking about you." After a few months, the letters became words that made flowing sentences. It was as if the universe was talking to me.

Around this time I went into a sort of slide. I felt a little lost one day, experiencing an overwhelming sadness. Lying on my lounge room carpet, tears rolling down my face, I couldn't understand why. My life was great!

Just then I heard a squawking noise and the blinds on my lounge room window began to move. A large bird appeared and flew around the room. I have always been afraid of birds caught in rooms with no apparent way out, but it managed to fly back out through the blinds and was gone. As I pulled back the blind to look outside, there on the window sill was a beautiful rainbow lorikeet, one of Australia's native birds. This little fellow was predominantly green in color with splashes of yellow, red and white. He didn't move when he saw me; he just cocked his head to one side and weighed me up!

He looked at me for the longest time; I didn't move nor did he. I could almost hear him say "What's going on here?" My tear stained face may have explained to a human, but to a bird, I wasn't so sure. This little bird seemed to understand. It was one of those magical moments when time stands still and you know you are experiencing something very special!

Very slowly, I moved closer to the little bird. He didn't move. I grabbed some bread from the kitchen and held it close to his beak. He ate it. When I brought back more, he jumped right onto my finger and ate it straight from my hand. Feeling his tiny feet on my finger, I also felt the trust in this little creature, and for the first time in my life I felt the connection. I truly felt the connection that told me we are all part of the one giant thing that holds us all together, though we are all so different. We are not separate at all. I had known this in theory but in that moment, I felt it.

When he finally flew away I sat on my sofa, and as I did, the room filled with hundreds of tiny sparks, flitting and darting about like tiny diamonds in the air. It took my breath away. I had never seen anything like it before. I clearly heard the words in my head "You are never alone." I named the little bird Paulie and he came everyday, bringing his friends and family.

A couple of years later, my daughter and I had moved a short distance to Mosman, home to our famous Taronga Park Zoo. Around this time, I decided to try this new line of thought that everyone was talking about. I made a statement to the universe with conviction. "I'm ready to live with a man once again. I'm ready!" As we all know, the universe never fails to deliver, and shortly thereafter my Dad arrived at the door with his bags, asking me if he could stay. Ah yes, the universe does have a wicked sense of humor and my statements needed some fine tuning. I'd forgotten to mention "in a romantic way."

It was in this new location that I decided to tackle the walk down to Balmoral Beach, a steeply-sloped hill down to the water and a monumental walk back up! I forced myself up at 5:30 one morning and donning joggers, track pants and T shirt, started the steep walk from my apartment down to the water. The peaceful view from the top of the slope was magnificent, with the rocky outline of the shoreline and Manly Bay across the water. People jogging past me all looked very fit, with their dogs on leashes, or babies in pushchairs with Dads at the helm. This was a whole new world to me, a little culture all of its own. Everyone was smiling and saying "Hello" or "Good morning." This was lovely! At the bottom of the slope, I walked along the shore, taking in the Balmoral Bathers Pavilion, the club on the water where the 'old boys' start their swim every morning, rain or shine. I continued past the rotunda where *Shakespeare by the Sea* takes place on warm summer evenings, down past the coffee shops and restaurants to the rock pools at the very end. I was living someone's dream… mine!

As I walked each morning before first light, I would admire the manicured gardens, hear the birds singing and catch sight of the rabbits in the bushes around the park. This was a very different world. As I walked back up the steep hill (very slowly with lots of pauses) other people would pass by me running up. Wishing I was that fit, I put that goal out there to be able to run up like them.

I walked every day, until one day while wishing I could run up like the others, I stopped half way up and looked back down to the beach. At that stage I was walking up and down sometimes twice a day without stopping. A thought struck me. "We never stop long enough to see how far we have come. We look around at others ahead of us, and plan for something ahead as a goal, but how often do we stop and think how far we have come?"

In not doing so, we miss something important. We feel we are missing out by not reaching that goal just yet. We miss enjoying the success of being so much further on than we were. And when we stop to look back… What a view! At the top of the slope that morning I happened to look up at a sign right next to me that had always been there. I smiled when I read the message: "Awake season. Are you ready?"

Yes I think I am!

Once again it was time to move (must be the gypsy heritage). I stayed with a friend for a few months while trying to find the right place. At that time, my girlfriend gave me a book to read by Florence Scovell Shin, a compilation of four books. Florence was a metaphysical teacher in the early 1900s. Her books are easy to understand and her teachings so simple to put into place. In one chapter, Florence explains how to manifest a new home. Write down all you would like it to be – size, rooms, location and price, and then give it up to the Creator. Then you have to give a big demonstration. For example: buy some new linen for your bed in your new home.

I wrote my list. Florence stated that you shouldn't think about how it will come together, just trust. I must say that doubt filled my mind when I thought of how much it would cost to have this home on my list. I couldn't see how it could happen, but I trusted. I went to the local market on Saturday and purchased a new white linen duvet set. I pictured it on my bed in my new home.

Three weeks later I found something almost exactly like my list, except I wanted a house in order to have a little dog, but this was an apartment. My girlfriend said "You are supposed to be trusting. Just wait." So I did. Two weeks later, a little house came up for lease. I couldn't believe the price. It had everything I wanted on my list and a garden, front and back.

I started to see that once I had let go of the how, things could happen in a better way than I ever imagined!

In this little house, I found contentment as I had never known it. The family had grown now, since Dad had become a permanent fixture. I had forgotten to state how many bedrooms I wanted so I had to sleep in the lounge. I didn't care; I had polished floor boards, a new kitchen with gas, French doors, and gardens with trees and plants. Heaven!

I had not really meditated at this point but after receiving a tape by Dr Doreen Virtue from my niece, I attempted it. I loved the process and immediately went off into a sort of Walt Disney world of colors and sensations. My mind was still and I felt so relaxed. Meditating every morning made me feel great. My days flowed; my relationships became richer. I became so aware of how rich my life was, and how blessed I was. I had four healthy children, a beautiful grandson, fantastic family and friends, a great house, car, job, but most of all, I had found my connection to the Creator of All That Is and I felt so alive and awake!

During one of my morning meditations, I was surprised to hear the voice of a little character – a fish, with an American accent. He spoke to me about life and how we don't use our intuition like the animals do, and how amused he was at how clever humans think they are. "Man, can you learn a thing or two from us!" he laughed. I came out of my meditation thinking "What is going on?" I have a fantastic imagination but the things this little fish was saying… I didn't know where it was coming from.

Allowing

*I am one with the earth
and all creation.*

*Just as a peaceful heart attracts the
earth's gentle creatures towards us,
Mother Earth makes her presence
known with great gentleness. The key
to moving into a state of awakened
perception is allowing ourselves to be
present, to move into harmony with
the gentleness of the natural world.*

I thought "This can't be a meditation. I am supposed to not think about anything," but this is what was happening, and even when I wasn't meditating he would talk to me wherever I was at the time, convenient or not. At this stage I started to write down everything he said. Once when I was a little out of sorts, he spoke to me as I drove to work out of the blue. He laughed "Sister you're looking hot today, ouch!" I couldn't help but laugh with him. He was so cheeky. "You're down today but that's 'cos you're not connecting to the source. Just like a light bulb; it's just a plain ol' light bulb, nothing going on, until you reach up and connect it to the source; then pow, illumination… and you see everything so clearly. Sister, this little light of mine I'm gonna let it shine. You know the words and right now its midnight around here, so connect up baby!"

I couldn't stop laughing. He was right; I felt out of sorts because I had forgotten to connect up. It was so simple. This little creature stayed with me for years. I wrote what he said on scraps of paper, backs of envelopes and time flew by. I wondered whether I should write this as a book, but I saw it as a movie.

This was synchronicity in action.

I told my children about it and they all said "Mum you have to write this stuff down" as did my friends. One had connections with the Australian makers of the movie "Happy Feet," but still I procrastinated. I saw it as a Disney movie.

Later the movie "Fish Tale" came out and I thought "Oh it's too late now," but it's never too late and my fish became a bird, a fantastic black bird called Jack. It was no coincidence that my first awakening to all this connectedness came through my little Rainbow Lorikeet Paulie, all those years ago. Jack brought lots of other characters to see me (at present under wraps) and a story finally became complete. I was still thinking Disney, not sure how to approach them, but trusting…

I moved once again, still in Mosman, down towards the ferry and Mosman Bay – an idyllic, small Federation building with tall ceilings, open space and a back garden, this time full of tame rabbits. Along came the Rainbow Lorikeets and the Kookaburras, not forgetting the Ring tale Possum, to our new home in paradise.

One night after a very sociable get together in the garden with our neighbors, I talked to them about my movie idea. Would you believe it? One of my neighbor's brothers was CEO of Fox Studios and two of the others worked for…wait for it, Walt Disney. It came to my door! I was in complete amazement as this group of neighbors listened and laughed at the antics of these little characters saying "You have to do something with this stuff!"

I am.

While all of this was happening, I experienced my first conscious awareness of clairaudience. I was in the kitchen of my little house making a sandwich when I heard a lady whisper in my ear. I was too frightened to turn around as Dad was standing to my left and I knew we were alone. The lady's voice was soft and comforting. She told me not to be afraid, but I was still aware that no one else was there. The lady asked me to write down what she was saying so I had to find some paper quickly. Dad looked at me oddly but I kept writing. The lady told me lots of things about herself and my boyfriend and things to tell him. The lady was my boyfriend's mother who had passed years before. My boyfriend had told me very little about her and was quite the skeptic.

Some time later I told him what had happened. When I gave him the information, he asked me what color her eyes where, but I couldn't remember what she had said. "Oh I would have believed all of this if you had known that one thing," he said. I found the piece of paper I had written my notes on at home and gave it to him. He gasped; her eyes were blue. I said "I don't know." He said "You wrote it down." I was shocked.

I finally started to accept that all of these things were happening because I was awake – to my connection and my life on both the physical and spiritual planes. It is nothing short of miraculous and magical! And it all began here, on the lower North Shore of Sydney…

My beautiful niece introduced me to Sophia Fairchild on International Angel Day in 2009. I thought Sophia was an angel. I also met Simon Wing Lun there, a Theta Practitioner who introduced me to ThetaHealing. I loved it so much that I became a Theta Practitioner myself. Now I am contributing with the other beautiful souls writing this book. I am blessed!

I have learnt that the Universe, the Creator of All That Is, never gives up on us, is there to open doors, light the way and keep us connected. No matter where we are, we are all students and teachers to each other throughout life.

Connecting with the Creator
ThetaHealing is wonderful modality of healing; it allows us instant access to the 7th plane of existence where we can ask the Creator what's going on at anytime about any issue. We learn to 'Go up and ask God' by means of meditation. The answers we are given let us look inside ourselves to see how events, nature/nurture, beliefs, past, present, other lifetimes have led us to think of ourselves in a certain way and act accordingly, thereby creating circumstances in our lives that mirror those beliefs back to us. (Usually in a negative way.)

We learn how this has served us (it always has in some way) and how we can change the beliefs that really haven't served us by asking the Creator to give us his perspective of the issue for our highest good. We also ask the creator to download new feelings into us, feelings that we may not have experienced before. Once you experience a beneficial feeling you can attract more of it, like feeling loved.

I have found that the easiest way to connect with the Creator/Universe is to start each day with a meditation. Even when it appears that I have limited time, that's when I need to meditate the most.

My meditations can be for 2 – 4 minutes, but the longer you can spend in meditation, the more open you will be to divine communication and ultimately to peace.

Lie down and relax.

Take 3 deep breaths slowly and exhale slowly. Feel yourself going inwards.

Picture yourself inside a ball of white, iridescent light, coming up from the earth's center, cleansing and balancing as it travels up through the red (root) chakra; cleansing and balancing it travels up through the orange (sacral) chakra; cleansing and balancing it travels up through the yellow (solar plexus) chakra; cleansing and balancing it travels up through the green (heart) chakra; cleansing and balancing it travels up through the light blue (throat) chakra; cleansing and balancing it travels up through the dark blue (third eye) chakra; cleansing and balancing it travels up through the violet (crown) chakra.

Now see the ball of light coming out through the top of your head as it continues going up and out into the universe, past the white lights… dark lights… white lights… then up through the jelly-like substance that are the laws. And as the ball dissolves, move towards the white light and enter it.

This is known as the 7th plane of existence, the plane from which all things are manifested. Spend some time in this place, where clarity is gained and truths made known. It is a peaceful, joyful place, full of wisdom and grace.

When you are ready to return, send your energy consciousness through the same sequence in reverse. When you reach the earth's center, bring your energy consciousness back up into your space. This is called grounding.

I have a shortcut these days so that I can visualize this process at any time. I put my thumb and forefinger together and close my eyes for a second. This is my way of instantly connecting up to the Creator of All that Is/The Universe for instant guidance.

When I am in the 7th plane, there are times when I ask lots of questions. The answers I receive are not always what I would like to hear, but they are always wise and profound. Sometimes they make me laugh and more often than not, lead me to question myself further.

I find that in life, people generally don't take the time to just stop for long enough to find out what's really going on for them. Meditation allows us to stop focusing on the illusion of life and go inward to find the truth, to connect with our higher selves and all of creation.

This is the place to really co-create the life we are meant to live. The answers are always there!

Human Relationships

I am related to all that is.

*All of our relationships make up
our tribe, including our relations
with spirit helpers and animal allies.
By building bonds of intimacy, sharing
life experiences, laughing with loved
ones, together we create enduring
harmony within the greater
human tribe.*

LAURA BESSAN
São Paulo, Brazil

IN HER LATE TWENTIES, with a Bachelor Degree in Economic Science and an M.B. in International Business from NYU, Laura thought she had everything a modern woman could dream of. She had a very successful career working for an International Company, a husband, nice apartment and traveled all around the world. But she was not happy.

After her first pregnancy, it became clear that something needed to change. Her spiritual journey began with Flower Essence Therapy, and with her second pregnancy, she was ready to give up her executive career.

Laura knew that a new life direction had arrived when the book *Sacred Space* by Denise Linn was placed in her hands. Moved by inner insight, she flew to the United States to study with the author. On returning to Brazil, Laura began her work healing spaces. However, she continued to study and has incorporated many different techniques into her work, such as aromatherapy, flower essence therapy, dowsing, radionics and geobiology. Becoming a certified Soul Coach finally completed her knowledge of harmonization of both people and environments.

Over the years, Laura has conducted consultancies for individuals, homes and businesses, facilitating workshops and seminars. She now works with teenagers and young adults, coaching them to discover their talents, passions and abilities, to understand their aspirations and frustrations, providing them with a safe environment where they can follow their hearts and choose the role they wish to play on our planet.

Contact Laura by Email at Lbessan@uol.com.br

The Ultimate Sign

LAURA BESSAN

*I knew it was time to rely on Divine Intelligence: time to allow
the natural cycle of life and death to flow without interference.*

*I*t was spring time in Brazil in the first week of October, 2000. The sun had
risen earlier and a blue sky had appeared with the first rays of the sun. I was
looking towards the Atlantic forest right behind our summer-house.

The forest looked greener because of the mixture of blue skies and streaks of
rose and golden light passing through branches and leaves. Noisy parrots were
playing and welcoming the glorious morning. A pair of toucans rested peacefully
in front of the back window.

We lived in São Paulo, Brazil, the richest city in the country, with 11 million
habitants. So whenever I came to our beach house I felt a reconnection with the
earth, to its rhythms, to inner peace. As I slowly prepared the breakfast, I gave
thanks for the life I had, for the wonderful day outside, for my body, my kids,
my husband, for the sacred country that I had chosen to embody in this life time.

Movement gradually began to stir in the house. The maid came back after
walking the dog. The kids woke up and settled on the couch waiting for something to eat. Our two children, a boy 10 years old and a girl 4 years old, were on
their spring break holidays from school. We had traveled to our summer house
in Bertioga on the sea coast of São Paulo to enjoy seven days of tranquility, close
to nature at the beach.

My husband Mateo remained in the city working. He lived to work. He'd
sometimes jokingly say that his priorities in life were the company he worked for,
our kids, the soccer team he supported and me. Though he placed me last on the
list, deep in my heart I knew he was only joking.

The telephone rang. Mateo was not well. He had fainted during a company
meeting and been taken to the hospital. As I spoke to him over the phone his voice
was low. I tried to remain calm though my heart was beating crazily. He had felt
a very strong pain in his stomach, and then lost consciousness.

I hung up the phone and glanced at the children, trying not to reveal my
concern. I told them I had to go back to São Paulo to solve some problems and

asked the maid to sleep over to take care of them. An hour and a half later I was at the hospital.

Though Mateo looked very pale, he claimed to be well. He had undergone several medical examinations and the cardiologist reported the diagnosis: Stress! He should take some time away from work to rest.

We were so relieved. Mateo phoned the office and advised he would be taking two days off. We returned to our beach house that same day. However, Mateo kept on working the whole time we spent there.

The week of our spring break flew by. We were back in town on Monday. The children returned to school. As usual Mateo went into the office and resumed working frenetically. Being an executive in the financial markets, he could never unplug.

I had given up the corporate world in 1995 and immersed myself deeply into the spiritual world. At that time, I was doing Interior Alignment® and Intuitive Feng Shui, working and teaching people to balance their lives through their home environments.

Life went on. Autumn had already begun. Although the climate is warm in South America, we could feel the chilly wind and see the leaves drifting down from the trees.

Mateo was very thin. He had always been slim and athletic, but he had lost an unusual amount of weight in recent months. I had not forgotten that strange fainting episode in the spring. So I insisted almost daily that he go for a check-up.

On May 10th he had finally scheduled the check-up, expecting to be back in his office by noon. I called his cell phone several times but had no answer. When he called me, he said they had found a minor problem in his stomach, nothing to worry about and that they wanted him to return for another examination. But he postponed this until after an important business trip to Italy. When Mateo took this examination after returning from Europe, I was in my home office writing a report.

The telephone rang. It was the doctor from the hospital speaking.

"Your husband has cancer in his stomach, stage four. We needed to talk!"

As I hung up the phone I had the impression that this was not happening! It seemed as though a movie was passing by in front of my eyes. My life became a hurricane after that phone call.

It had been 20 years since I met Mateo. Our first years together were full of love, joy and lightness. He always looked after me. Of course we had our disagreements, but we always overcame everything together.

After the birth of our first child, Mateo had become very demanding of me. He began to delegate all household expenses to me. He was slowly passing over to me the entire control of his salary, and educating me in financial matters. Though I didn't understand why, I complied. He always justified this by saying that he was too busy working and he needed my help to make his life easier. I never thought that one day I would begin to understand why.

On May 31, after 10 hours of surgery, the doctors took out the duodenal cancer and part of his stomach, part of his pancreas, part of his liver, gallbladder and small intestine. The diagnosis was only six months to live.

When he began the weekly chemotherapy sessions, I was always with him. Although there have been many advances in the field of cancer treatment, the places where cancer therapy happens are sad and quiet. Yet – our love and energy had grown. We felt so strong, full of hope and open to all possibilities, that when we arrived at the treatment room, the energy instantly changed. People would come and talk to us, and we always had a hopeful word so they would leave feeling renewed and full of faith.

Mateo listened to a tape of healing meditations during all of his chemotherapy sessions. He started to change. I think he began to gradually understand what had transformed me into a more loving, compassionate and peaceful person. He now accepted alternative therapies. He went to a flower essence therapist and started using orthomolecular medicine.

One year after the first diagnosis, the levels of cancer cells in Mateo's blood had not decreased. The chemotherapy sessions had only weakened him more. In addition, the lack of half his digestive system organs meant that he was unable to completely absorb the food he ate. Although he was working every day, Mateo was now very thin and had started exhibiting strange symptoms. His left leg didn't function properly and he felt unbalanced walking.

When the doctor ordered a CT brain scan, they discovered a lemon-sized tumor in the frontal right lobe of his brain.

We had driven to the hospital in two cars and now were returning home in separate vehicles. It is very common in a big city like São Paulo to have vendors selling goods at the traffic lights. Mateo's car had come to rest just behind mine waiting for the traffic light to turn green. Thus a flower seller hit my car window with two packs of red roses. The small note from Mateo read: "You have been the light of my life, now you are also the source of my energy. I love you!" Tears flooded from my eyes, but in my heart I knew that everything that happens in our lives is for the greater good. At that moment I didn't have a clue why…

The surgery was quickly scheduled. After 16 hours, the tumor was removed and the left side of his body was paralyzed. We returned home five days later. Mateo was walking with difficulty, using a cane to support himself. He was completely dependent on me to use the stairs of our house. He was slimmer and very depressed. I was very sad. It was so difficult for me to see my man and the father of my children unable to live a complete life.

It was spring again. After a month of physical therapy, Mateo was able to move by himself and drive again. He had never once complained of his condition; at no time did I feel that he had given up. He was a strong man and somewhere inside, the warrior was ready for the next battle.

The diagnosis was the same; he had just six months to live. By now, Mateo had begun to decelerate. He kept going to the office every day, but was only working a few hours.

By this time, he became deeply immersed in his transformation. He attended radiotherapy sessions every day. Although he lost his hair completely and his body and external looks were entirely different, his light was growing and he was more attractive to me than ever before.

He continued receiving flower therapy by phone and began taking Jin Shin Jitsu sessions at home. Jin Shin is a technique to balance the body's energy, optimizing health and enhancing our own healing ability. Jin Shin Jitsu helped Mateo to reconnect with his love essence. Through working as an executive for many years he had learned to be a leader, giving orders and directing others, keeping his love essence detached. Now, at the end of each session, everyone could see that he was shifting his energy and turning into a more loving person.

His sensitivity was acute. We always had many friends, but with the progression of his disease, very few people stuck around, except for our family and two or three friends. I couldn't understand their silence and distance. I felt abandoned. Mateo gathered all his wisdom to tell me: "People stay away because it is very difficult for human beings to face their own mortality."

Mateo returned one day from the office devastated. He had to dismiss an employee who was not achieving the company goals. Firing people was part of his work. However this time the person involved was very angry, attacking him verbally: "It is no coincidence that you have cancer; you are an insensitive man." Despite the harshness of those words, Mateo was able to reflect on his past acts and perhaps understand the reason for his existence. The next day, he offered up a prayer asking for forgiveness, forgiving himself and releasing that person.

Although we didn't talk about it, I was feeling that Mateo's physical body could not withstand any more sessions of chemotherapy and radiation. The cancer cells were multiplying at great speed. Our major concern was the kids.

The children were now going to a flower essence therapist weekly. During one session, my daughter created a drawing of the family together, holding hands. Our feet were all touching the ground except Mateo's. He was already going to another dimension, and she had noticed.

Regeneration

*Every ending marks
a new beginning.*

Nothing is ever truly lost; energy simply transforms. Though the light may be hidden, it still shines. There is a homecoming even in a time of loss. Through tears and laughter, truth is revealed, relationships are strengthened. We move forward with grace, hope and love.

With deep sadness in my heart, I called two friends who had been dowsing to help Mateo overcome the disease. I asked them to stop. His life was too painful here. He needed to leave. He had lost mobility and his physical body was suffering. I knew it was time to rely on Divine Intelligence; it was time to allow the natural cycle of life and death to flow without interference.

After that, Mateo spent almost every day at home, only going to the office for a few meetings. At home he was the father he had never been. He spent long afternoons playing with the kids, helping them with their homework.

In the meantime, I was invited to give a speech for an Interior Alignment® and Intuitive Feng Shui Seminar in Brazil. This was a great challenge for me. I had worked with both techniques for six years, had built up an excellent reputation as a consultant and a list of over 600 clients, but I was still terrified of public speaking.

Mateo had been so devoted to his work that he had no idea how my business was going. When I told him about my invitation to speak at the seminar he gave me full support. He had extensive experience in public speaking including in other languages. He not only helped me to prepare my computer presentation, he trained me in speech and posture, gave me tips on how to look at the audience and made me feel absolutely secure. The seminar took place at the beginning of June to an audience of over 200 people and it was an absolute success.

I had the impression that Mateo held himself steady until the seminar was over. Then he got worse. His headaches grew more intense and he was admitted to hospital. This last diagnosis was: the cancer had taken over all his organs, including his spinal fluid. Nothing more could be done.

From that moment on I could only cry. He quietly asked me to go back home. I had arranged to send the kids to our beach house; I thought it would be too traumatic for them to stay at home watching their father die. The children were ready to travel when we got home.

Mateo was in a wheelchair, too weak to stand. The kids were frightened to see their father this way, but he was serene. He told them that everything would be fine and that he loved both of them more than anything in the world. Once they left the room, he finally melted into tears, saying: "I'm going to miss you."

Our next days together were eternal. Time had slowed down. We spent every moment together, mostly in silence. We had built an intensive care unit inside our home and I had hired two nurses to help with intravenous feeding and the injectable drugs. But I never left his side. Each morning I shaved him and combed the little hair he had. Although the doctors had diagnosed on two occasions that Mateo only had six months to live, he had lived another two years. And I wouldn't trade this time for any other 20 years we had together.

I see couples living together today without ever experiencing love as a connection of mind, body and spirit. Perhaps that is the reason behind the frenetic search for a soul mate. I believe the soul mate lives in any other human being you have attracted into your life. He or she has the exact qualities and defects that are necessary for your evolution. When you can recognize them in yourself, you are able to transform and balance your own male and female forces, living a full love story.

My mother stayed with us for weeks; she was our guardian angel. She took care of our house, helped with the shopping and preparing special foods. One morning Mateo asked her to go out of the room and leave us alone.

He said: "I want to ask you two things. The first one is that I want you to go to the hairdresser to dye your hair. I don't like it when you don't take care of yourself.

Secondly, you have to take back the promise you made when we got married: that I was and would be the only man in your life."

It felt like a punch in my stomach. How could I go back on a promise like that? I quickly answered, "You're crazy! I can't do it."

"You are wrong," he said. "You can and you will do it. You are a young and very beautiful woman and still have a long life to live. Being alone, you will become bitter. Also, I'm thinking of the kids. They still have to learn more about the role of men in the world, and you cannot teach it to them! You are a woman… a strong woman," he added.

"But Mateo, I love you and do not want another man with me," said I.

"I know you love me and because I love you and the kids more than my own life I want you to withdraw the promise. Also, I promise that if I can, I will help you choose a new partner. I don't know what will happen after I'm gone, but if it is possible, I will send you a signal when you've found the right person."

"I can't believe you. Even in such a situation, you can plan all these details…" I argued.

"Then stop reeling and promise me that you will try to be happy again," he ordered.

I didn't want to argue with him. So I made the promise, thinking that I would not have the chance to fulfill it.

"Can I ask you something?" I said.

"What?"

"You know this thing about signs? You know how I'm afraid of dying? So, if the other side of the veil is nice and safe, will you send me a sign?" I asked.

"We have an agreement! I've always believed that by abandoning all fear of death it is possible to be born and reborn again," he replied.

That afternoon when I returned from the hairdresser Mateo was asleep, and slept for the next two days.

I awoke on a rainy Thursday morning. When I entered the room where Mateo was lying unconscious, I noticed something was different. Although it was raining outside, there was a bright light all over the room. His face was very serene, and it looked as if a small thread of light was rising out of his solar plexus. His spiritual body was leaving the worldly dimension. I knew it would not be too long before the physical body would be declared dead.

I spent the day at his side reading and praying. I witnessed his dying process as a dancing thread of lights radiating from his entire body. It was like heaven receiving the light of their child. The room was filled with angelic beings all day long and at 6 o'clock in the afternoon he had gone, silently, gently and in a holy peace.

The next day, the children returned from the beach house. I told them that their father had gone and that from that day on, we would be a family of three. But I was absolutely certain that their father would protect us from wherever he was.

The ceremony and burial took place in a Brazilian cemetery. After speaking with the children, I went to Mateo's funeral. I don't remember too many details. It was a very cold day. The sky was completely blue and when it all ended, I looked up at the sky and there was a letter *M* drawn in thin, white clouds!

I lived in grief, loneliness and isolation for the next several months. I didn't want to see or talk to anyone. The children were my only support and companionship and I cried every single day.

One day, my son, then aged twelve, wiping my tears said: "I don't think wherever dad is, he is happy to see you crying every day!"

At this point I said to my heart: enough. Life went on and I tried to occupy myself working with the Soul Coaching® techniques.

Nine months after Mateo's death, as I was leaving our home, I discovered a red rose placed at the door step. It was our wedding anniversary.

Everything that happened through this significant life experience has brought me profound lessons. I have learned that we should not qualify the events of our lives as good or bad. The universe is completely connected, allowing us to live every second of our existence with lightness, love and assistance. I have learned to have resilience, adjusting to life's circumstances, focusing on gains rather than losses, and appreciating the blessings I have received.

The only true thing we know is the present moment. And sometimes the physical body can't be healed. However, in such cases, the cure happens at the soul's level and for this reason it is necessary to make the transition. Death is only a rebirth back into spirit.

One year after his death, a friend of Mateo's called me. He had just divorced from an unhappy marriage, and after talking several times by phone we decided to go out for dinner. It was a quiet meal. We talked about everything, however it seemed as though we had known each other forever. He was gentle, loving and caring.

As we were leaving the restaurant he looked at my pointy-toed shoes and said jokingly: "Did you kill a cockroach in the corner of the room with the tip of your shoes?" I could only smile.

It was the sign! Mateo had made this exact comment to me a couple of years earlier!

Meditation for the Healing Process
Sit silently and close your eyes.
Start to breathe deeply.

Imagine yourself walking along a small road. It has just stopped raining.
The wind is slowly dispersing all the clouds and the sky is becoming blue again.
Rays of sunshine are slowly appearing.
The wet ground brings the scent of the earth to your nose.

After walking for a few minutes, you begin to hear the sound of running water very close by. You can see a bridge over the crystal waters of a river and, crossing it, you will enter into a beautiful garden.

It's your secret garden, a place only you know. It is surrounded by large trees, all covered with damp leaves, flowers and butterflies happily fluttering across a small lake.

The sun's rays pierce the leaves and branches and point out a chair, all turned into pure emerald, a special throne. It is as if the chair invites you to sit on it. You walk toward it and sit comfortably.

Keep on breathing deeply. You are safe here; just relax and enjoy.
The energy of the sunlight weaves through the tall trees.
Leaves and flowers are drifting down onto your body, and a pleasant, warm light envelopes you.

You can feel the crystalline light entering through your breath, entering through your nose, passing through your mouth, reaching your lungs, where a pure oxygen breath is carried into your heart.

Imagine this transparent and divine light being pumped from your heart into your bloodstream and bathing your organs one by one. Image all of your organs – the esophagus, stomach, pancreas, liver, gallbladder, duodenum, intestines, kidneys, bladder, reproductive system, the excretory apparatus – all receiving this crystalline light.

This glorious light shines into your immune system, your nervous system, all of its glands, pituitary, hypothalamus, thyroid, parathyroid, adrenals, pancreas and gonads and finally, your brain.

Your body lies in a sea of transparent, brilliant, transformative light.
Light cleanses you from all pain, all sorrow, all anger, every fear and any loneliness.
It cleanses all toxins from any food, drug and drinks you have ingested.
Imagine a new seed of life, opening up from the cleansing earth, starting over again.
You are a being of light.

Rays of translucent light rise out of your body, moving out through your eyes, your mouth, the palms of your hands, the soles of your feet, your skin and through the top of your head.
You are a being of light.

Now you are transformed into a big ball of energy and light and you will be mixing your energy with the earth, the plants, the water and all animals.
You are a being of light.

Your energy increases and goes beyond the garden and mixes with the sky and the sun.
You are a being of light.
And finally you blend into space, to infinity.
You are a being of light.

You have returned to the source of life.

You are one with the Creator.

We are all one. A great light. A great peace.

The only perfection, the total healing and wisdom exists within you. It exists within your own body.

Completely renewed, you gather all the light you need. You collect all the strength necessary to process your healing. You receive all knowledge to understand your life.

You go back through space, returning to planet earth.

You go back to your secret garden.

And slowly you return into your physical body.

Start making small movements in your extremities, opening and closing your hands, moving your feet, taking a deep breath, stretching your body and opening your eyes slowly.

You stand up from the emerald chair and start leaving your garden, your sacred space, your healing cocoon.

You walk across the bridge, crossing the river back to the little road where you began.

You're completely safe. Whenever you need to, you can come back to your garden.

You are a child of light.

You have been reborn.

You are the divine expression and perfection of the Creator.

☙

ANGELA TALARICO
Sudbury, Ontario, Canada

ANGELA TALARICO BECAME a certified Angel Therapy Practitioner® in 2010 after receiving guidance from her angels. She graduated from Laurentian University in 2001 and later from Humber College with International Marketing in 2002. She has been on a life long journey of spirituality and enjoys learning and growing in all ways possible. She tries to keep an open mind and heart at all times. Angela is a new mom to a beautiful little boy who inspires her every day and reminds her to stay in the present moment. She is in a committed relationship with her loving boyfriend of 9 years and father to Parker, Chad. She is a sister, daughter and pet owner to a Samoyed dog named Fonzie and her cats Toni and Alvin, but really recognizes that we are all just spirits on a human journey.

Angela started a small natural soap company called Sudsations in 2008, and spends her spare time making soap or cooking meals for her family. Angela enjoys walking in nature, animals, yoga and swimming in the ocean. She appreciates life in its simplest forms.

Angela works part time giving angel readings, and holds workshops from her hometown Sudbury Ontario. Visit her website: www.angeltherapist.org.

Moving Into the Light

ANGELA TALARICO

*There was something about being in this young forest that resonated with me.
It too was like a little baby, growing and flourishing into
something more magnificent as the seasons passed.*

My hometown, Sudbury, Ontario, is a mining town with a lot of black mountains and small trees. Life isn't bustling in our modest little part of the planet, but that's only if you are looking with your eyes. When you look with your heart, Mother Nature paints a very different picture. Our forest may be young, but its essence is powerful. Years ago, all vegetation was wiped out because of acid rain, leaving the land barren and the once gray-pink granite mountains black. By the 1950s, Sudbury's landscape was almost completely desolate. Our local mine eventually built a smoke stack to redirect the toxic fumes up into the atmosphere instead of directly onto the land. Not ideal conditions, but a much better solution.

Since then, Sudbury has implemented growth programs, which have resulted in our beautiful, youthful forest. It is the true Northern Ontario experience – evergreens, birch trees, pines, maples and cedars, growing along numerous water fronts, their colors and beauty truly breathtaking. It illustrates that even where life appears barren and dead, it can thrive. An underlying vitality surrounds our city, now bustling with the birth of new life. The trees may be small, but they are powerful and magnificent. It was here, in my hometown, where I first discovered my pregnancy.

I remember the day so clearly. The doctor entered the room, and said, "Well, you were right Ms. Talarico, something isn't right with your body. You're pregnant!" He congratulated me and left the room. I sat on the bed a moment longer, in a state of confusion and shock. This was really happening. I was pregnant! Me, pregnant! That was not was I was expecting. Anxiety flooded my entire being. I instantly wanted to be the best Mom, but worried that I may not be. The idea of having an entire life in my hands suddenly seemed like a huge responsibility. I needed to ground myself.

So, I began spending my afternoons in my favorite place. I longed to be in my sacred space in the forest to clear my mind. By connecting with the nature that Sudbury had to offer, all worries and stress of the world melted away. There was something about being in this young forest that resonated with me. It too was like a little baby, which was not only growing, but also flourishing into something more magnificent as the seasons passed. One thing I can always count on, when all else seems to be upside down, is the constancy of nature. Always changing and regenerating, nature infallibly offers balance to my turbulent emotions. I frequented the Laurentian Conservation Area; it was the only place where life made any sense to me, where I felt wholly at peace. I could feel the magic surrounding me, and for a miniscule portion of my day, I was. I simply *was*.

It was wintertime when the news of my pregnancy was revealed. I walked across the frozen lake into the forest on a beautiful sunny day. Sunshine filled me with warmth, love and a subtle sense of power. A warm, glowing, soft pink color radiated all around me in the forest. I observed the millions of different colors that glimmered like diamonds on the snow. Countless facets sparkled with brilliant intensity with each step I took. The surreal peachy pink color hovering slightly above the snow made me feel as if I was in a beautiful dream. Though the crisp air on my cheeks reminded me that I was not dreaming, there was a blurred line between reality and fantasy. The sky above was a clear, bright blue. I always felt peaceful while walking here.

I thought of the young trees that appeared dead during the winter. They however had little buds on their branches, growing and preparing to blossom in the spring. This was similar to the little bud in my belly, which was also not visible during this time, but still very much alive and growing. As I continued on, I heard her voice: "Continue to visit Nature to enjoy the many gifts she has to offer. Her energy is pure and can re-balance and re-generate your energy. Look to the trees for answers for they hold great wisdom. Sit with them and ask that they clear your chakra column. The silence that you hear is only with your outer ears. Listen with your heart and you will hear their words. Know that you are surrounded by love, and that you are love. I am with you to guide you; all you have to do is ask. Feel my presence and hear my soft words. You are a perfect child of God."

It was Ariel, the Archangel of nature. She was the first Divine being that I ever had conscious contact with. Pregnancy brought many spiritual gifts to me. My awareness of the oneness of life was heightened, especially out in the perfection of our young forest. My intuition had always been strong, and I'd always felt guided by an inner knowing. Over the years, I began to honor and follow these feelings, but even more significant were the feelings I had about this birth.

The moment I knew I was pregnant, I decided I wanted a midwife and a home water birth. This seemed fitting for me since I had a life-long phobia of hospitals, but absolutely loved being in water. However, when I voiced this decision, many people expressed their skepticism with a look of horror on their faces. I really didn't know how else to explain it; it just felt right to me.

When I met our team of midwives, it further solidified my decision. These were women who were completely aligned with my beliefs, and each visit felt like a breath of fresh air. Mary Eve was a beautiful redhead (like myself) who also frequented the conservation area, and I often bumped into her on the trails. Because it is rare to come across other people walking these trails, the nature of this synchronicity was validation to me. Mary Eve was the newest member of their team; it was a time of new beginnings for both of us. Leslie was calm, assertive and confident in her work. She had the ability to ease all my worries, reminding me that birth is a beautiful, natural process, and not something to be feared. Often during our meetings, we would discuss different topics related to spirituality, sometimes losing track of the time.

Springtime arrived, and there was a liveliness bursting all around me. The snow had melted and buds were beginning to unfold. The grass started to shoot through the earth. While flowers were awakening in the soil, preparing to bloom and share their beauty with the world, I marveled at how gracious and elegant nature was. I could appreciate God's handiwork, and just as the flowers were growing towards the light, so was I. I was recognizing the light within me and within all beings on this planet. As the seeds began sprouting, my own seed was also growing, and I nurtured it with love.

Springtime birthed new insight. Seeds of intention toward my life purpose were budding from deep within. A longing to make a difference in the world began to spark. I also felt a deep understanding of the death and birth cycles in this life. As my old 'selves' died off, a new self was emerging. No longer was I the party girl from university years, or the single hopeful. I was now stepping into a new phase, titled 'mother.' Still, regardless of personality, titles or outward appearances, I knew that none of this is who I really am. I treasured this experience and gave thanks for my beautiful blessing. I vowed to not lose my true self in this process, for I understood that I am spirit on my human journey and I also had my destiny to fulfill, as I awaited the full bloom of my own little bud.

Transformation was taking place all around me. Everything was awakening. Even the animals seemed livelier. Out in nature, the energy of the universe restored me, while Mother Earth awakened me. As I planted the seeds of intentions, I watched my seedlings grow and then blossom in harmony with All That Is.

Meanwhile, sometime after discovering my pregnancy, I began to connect with the soft and ever so sweet energy of Mother Mary. Her essence smelt faintly like fresh roses, and her energy was like a big hug. As I began working very closely with Mother Mary, she offered reassurance. "Sweet child, trust your instincts. A mother truly knows best. You have been making decisions without fully understanding why. Do not question these decisions. You are being guided. Your son is holy and perfect and he thanks you. He will be in your arms soon enough. Be patient and kind with yourself in the meantime. Rest when you need to. And remember you are surrounded by love. You are love, and you are of love. Peace and blessings to you my beautiful child." Her words, spoken like a true mother, reminded me to care for my vessel, honor my instincts and take time to rest.

As time passed, my faith wavered and I became discouraged by the stance that modern medicine takes: of birth being a medical procedure, rather than a miracle of life. I felt as if I was the only one who thought this was somewhat backwards. As the pregnancy progressed, I became even more disheartened as I continued to hear fear-based stories, and terrible accounts of the experience. Remarks of how brave I was for choosing a homebirth became the norm.

If '97–98% of babies are born healthy' why is birth something so feared in our society? Strangers would tell me to be prepared. My partner Chad had also received several warnings to not be offended by my erratic behavior during labor. Clearly alone with my beliefs, people would try to convince me that I was being naïve and that "I would see." Now, I'm not suggesting that the experience may have been less than enjoyable for some, it's just that I became enlightened to the reality that when you release any fear, there is no resistance and therefore, labor can be remarkably easy.

One day at work, a stranger approached me saying, "Oh my goodness, good luck! People might tell you it is not that bad, but it's worse than you can even imagine!" I could not believe that she had said that. Talk about things to never say to a pregnant woman! I shared these trials with my midwife during my next appointment, and once again she reassured me that everything would be perfect.

Leslie suggested I read a book called *Ina May and the Farm Midwives*. This book provides a completely different outlook on childbirth. It was written in the 1970s by a group of midwives, within a community of people living in caravans, surviving organically off their land. Although it was a book I wouldn't normally read, it became an amazing tool for me, and filled me with excitement about giving birth. The book may be outdated, yet its positive stories put a new spin on something that is normally viewed as a complication. I recommend this book as a gift to any woman who is pregnant. The accounts given of the natural births are all very positive, and the tone of the book is exactly what I needed. I became excited about giving birth again, as my mind frame grew even more positive. At last! These women who shared their experiences were all so optimistic!

Summertime soon arrived, as did new opportunities. Back in nature, my inner guidance was strong as I walked the trail I knew so well. It astonished me how beautiful yet different nature was at every stage of growth. I too was re-rooting myself into this planet. Summer was in full bloom, just like my belly and my thoughts. Guidance came daily and I journeyed from a fresh new perspective. At this point, I knew I needed to follow my guidance to travel to Hawaii. It was time to utilize my 'gifts' to help others rediscover and shine their own inner light in this world. My desire to make a difference was now stronger than ever. On that particular day, I walked up towards the mountainside cliff, which overlooks the vast fresh water lake and trees. On this cliff, as I sat and meditated, thoughts of the ocean and salt water filled my mind. I saw turquoise blue for as far as the eyes can see.

I've always felt connected to the ocean; it has always called to me. It signifies purity, well-being, change of life and being one with the flow. The rise and fall of the waves remind me of the ebb and flow of energy within my being. I love the smell of salt air, so fresh and regenerating. Perched high on the cliff in meditation, I could feel the purifying effects of the salt water on my skin, and running through my body into my blood stream. I visualized stepping into the ocean and feeling the cool sensation of being in the water, the soft sand moving through my toes. The experience was so vivid I could taste the salty ocean air in my mouth and a sense of longing filled my being. That day, as I left the conservation area, I stopped on the mountainside and watched the mesmerizing dance of sunlight moving and changing shapes, dancing across the water.

At my next appointment, Leslie told me I had inspired her during her summer vacation. She said she saw me as a gorgeous mermaid, stuck in a whirlpool, swirling downward, but I was rising up towards the light. She painted this image of me on a silk scarf and gifted it to me after the birth. This was yet another beautiful reminder of how in tune she was with me. It was a clear representation of what I was going through during this stage of my pregnancy. I had feelings of being overwhelmed and disconnected which could only be balanced in nature, mostly by water. Leslie instinctively knew that I needed to be by the water to purify the anxiety I had been experiencing and allow balance to be restored.

So, in June, 5 months pregnant, I followed my guidance and traveled to Kona, Hawaii, alone. Kona, which is more commonly called "The Big Island," is a magical place, a warm and sunny climate filled with tropical forests and active volcanoes. It has

> ### Contentment
>
> *I am truly blessed.*
>
> *Our hearts find comfort in knowing we are part of much larger cycles of life. The blooming buds of spring and the summer games of children are followed by falling leaves and warm winter fires. As we share our many blessings, our inner joy radiates out to bless and balance everything we touch.*

an air of the Hawaiian goddess Pele with her fiery fury, undertoned with a calm, peaceful energy. Doreen Virtue refers to the island as if you're on a giant crystal, and I can attest to this. After a long journey on three different flights and 18 hours of travel, I finally arrived in Kona. Completely exhausted, I was more than ready to get to the hotel, but there was magic in the air.

As I had stepped off the plane onto Hawaiian soil, a sense of complete peace came over me. I felt instantly relaxed and my mind switched to a trance-like state. Unfamiliar with this energy at the time, I enjoyed my newfound sense of tranquility. My cab driver was in no hurry either. As he slowly drove along the two lane highway, I began to wonder how many angry drivers would be tailing us at this slow speed. But to my surprise, no one seemed bothered by his relaxed driving. I knew then that I was definitely in paradise.

The week was deeply spiritual and I became a certified Angel Therapy Practitioner®. I was able to connect with like-minded individuals and to contact and work with many angels. I also met amazing healers and energy workers from many different fields, made incredible friendships and received a phenomenal amount of healing myself.

My time in Hawaii flew by, and on the last day of my journey in paradise, I went for a swim with the dolphins. I was awestruck by their energies and auras. Rainbows surrounded them and surprisingly, they traveled in little families. I noticed many couples with small babies. How cute they were! I floated in the water with the intention of connecting with them. As the groups swam past me, one baby dolphin swam upward and faced my belly. I could feel its loving rainbow healing energy surrounding me, and I knew the dolphins were communicating with my unborn baby. It was something I will never forget.

Summer passed and autumn arrived. Nature truly puts on a spectacular show during this season. I felt my energy shift and my connection to nature amplified. Fall is my favorite time of year, but this year it had particular meaning since the birth was also near. Outside I took deep breaths and felt the cool, crisp, clean air filling my entire being, and allowed it to fuel me with energy. I felt connected and secure, with a sense of wellbeing I've never known before. I experienced joy and gratitude throughout my body, as I walked with a newfound confidence in myself and my destiny. I trusted that the universe was taking care of us, and that everything would be OK.

That day, Quan Yin appeared in a mesmerizing swirl of reddish pink energy and offered her advice: "Faith, courage and strength are required for the next leg of your journey. Know that everything is as it should be, and you are fully receptive to the gifts that are being bestowed upon you. You are capable and powerful. Allow this energy to flow through you and great things will follow!"

October 6th, the morning I went into labor, was absolutely surreal. I immediately called on the goddess Diana for strength. Then, we called the midwife to give her the heads up, but I didn't think we would need her right away. I practiced staying mindful of the situation and focused all of my energy on relaxing and surrendering to the pain. My daily meditation practice helped me to stay focused, in a peaceful yet excited frame of mind. I felt a strong urge to be in water, so I immediately took a sea salt bath, where I listened to a Hypno-birth CD to balance the chakras, and to open up and relax my mind and body in preparation for birth. I was able to connect with my son, keeping in the forefront of my mind that he was on his way! The midwife wasn't due yet, but she decided to check in on me anyway.

When she came over, I was just stepping out of the bath. Pleased to see me so calm, Mary Eve examined me and said "Angela, you're fully dilated!" My calmness unraveled and I panicked because we had nothing prepared. As I lay on my bed, Mary Eve told me that I could push whenever I was ready. No way! I insisted I wanted to be in the water, and I wouldn't do it any other way. Some may call it bull headedness, but I prefer determined.

So, Chad and his mother grabbed buckets and began frantically filling the birthing pool in our living room. All the while, Mary Eve, my mother and sister stayed by my side. Mary Eve's energy during the birth was like Mother Mary's. She was completely sweet, compassionate and serene. Her soft touch conveyed her calm energy and allowed my body to fully relax.

Energy was intensified during the birth, and certain people would send me into frenzy. My partner was so excited and nervous that when he ran over to comfort me, the instant his hand touched any part of my body, I would feel a surge of his nervous energy rush through me, and my composure would instantly unravel. Luckily he was busy filling the pool. So, I continued to connect with my son, the goddess Diana, and Archangel Gabriel who is the protector of young children.

After about 45 minutes of waiting, they let me know that the pool was ready. Chad and I got in the pool. This was it: show time! It was time to shift my concentration from surrendering and opening, to pushing. Within 30 minutes of being in the tub, my son Parker was born

The moment of birth was the most mind-altering moment of my life. I made sure to keep my eyes open as my baby emerged. I was able to see the energy in the room as a swirl of whirling colors and waves. I was instantly grateful and euphoric as Parker was placed right on my chest. He didn't cry; he lay on my breast, looking at Chad and I. So Divine! Chad worried about his silence and cried out "Is he breathing?" Soon after, our son looked at us and let out his first cry, putting us both at ease.

How could something so miraculous and amazing be something so greatly feared? My desire to be in water was so profound, and I was so happy that I honored it. The birth was perfect: no complications, no tearing. From first contraction to birth was just over 5 hours. It was the most beautiful experience of my life, and I know this was because I followed my instincts and worked to release all fear.

And now, my journey through pregnancy is over. Everything I worked up to so diligently for the last 9 months has ended. He's finally here. I can only stop and wonder – now what? Talk about learning to live in the moment! The journey to birth has ended, but really it has all only just begun…

How to Open and Activate your Heart to Connect with Nature

First, find a secluded place in nature where you feel safe, comfortable and at peace. Sit under a tree with your spine resting on the trunk, as trees have the ability to rebalance our chakras. Be sure to ask for their permission to do this first. Once you have decided on your sacred space, call on your angels and guides to bless and clear the area. Trust that you will be safe and protected during this meditation.

Next, set your intention for this meditation to connect with the energy of nature.

Now, allow yourself to relax. Take a deep breath in, and gently release, out through your mouth. Allow your body to completely let go of any tension and worries, out into the universe with each exhale. Take another deep breath in, and gently and fully release out. Begin to breathe as you normally would, and allow yourself to find your rhythm.

Permit any thoughts that enter to drift out, as gently as they appeared. Simply let them go as gently as they entered. For in this time, we are connecting with the silent observer of these thoughts. Notice that you aren't your thoughts.

Now focus on a tiny glowing light in the center of your chest. Feel your heart center opening like a beautiful flower. Feel this as you inhale. The light grows, and on the exhale; it grows so large that it fills your entire being. Every organ, cell, muscle, tissue… your entire body is shining bright with light. It grows even larger to fill your aura. You are now glowing, a spectacular, shimmering white light. Feel the energy of the light. Sense your connection to all things.

Now, visualize roots spreading out from your root chakra into the earth beneath you. See these roots growing deep beneath the soil, passing through underground streams and deep into the center of this planet. Begin to draw up the energy of the earth through these roots with each breath. Feel this energy spreading upwards until it fills with the earth energy. Take this moment to give thanks for all that you are blessed with.

Now, the energy of the earth swirls and moves through your entire being. Visualize this energy pouring out of your heart chakra back to Mother Earth. See the planet in front of you as this energy fills and surrounds the earth. With each inhale, draw the energy in. Exhale and see or feel this love pouring back into Mother Earth.

Know that in this moment you are grounded and fully connected to your true self, and this planet. You are one with all that is, all that ever was, and all that will be. You are pure love. Feel it. See it. Send your blessings and gratitude to Mother Earth. You can sit here for as long as you like.

When you feel ready, become aware of your surroundings again. Gently wiggle your toes and fingers; feel your body once again and very slowly, open your eyes. You have now activated your heart, and connected with your true self, nature and All That Is.

You can do this meditation as often as you wish to strengthen your conscious bond with nature.

As I recognize the light within me, I recognize the light within you. Namaste.

∽

Equilibrium

I am perfectly relaxed and at peace.

*When all the elements within
and without are balanced, we arrive
at perfect equilibrium, a state of
suspended potential. There is wisdom
in waiting. The wise take joy in
allowing the vehicle to rejuvenate
before the next cycle of
creativity begins.*

KERRIE REDGATE
Sydney Australia

KERRIE REDGATE IS a specialist astrologer with 25 years of clinical experience, based in 35 years of research and study. As a practising Buddhist, Kerrie uniquely incorporates Buddhist Yogacara Psychology into her astrological work, elaborating on various levels of 'mind'. Her earlier studies of Taoism led naturally to an interest in Feng Shui, its links to astrology, and the powerful effects of 'place'. Astrology has been a major key in Kerrie's research into Reincarnation (sparked by her own early memories), leading also to studies of 'mind' and 'brain' within a spiritual context.

A Flower Essence Therapist since the mid-1980s, Kerrie has designed comprehensive flower essence formulas for healing various levels of *mind*. (You can find her chapter on flower essence birth charts in Ian White's book *Australian Bush Flower Healing*.)

Kerrie has taught innovative Astrology courses since 1991; has presented lectures to metaphysical, alternative-healing and conference groups; has been interviewed in-depth on Australian television and radio; and has been published in various magazines. She also teaches Reiki from the Buddhist perspective (a Sensei since 1997, and practitioner since 1986).

Kerrie primarily focuses on inspiring one's highest purpose, and the recognition and dissolution of specific self-sabotage patterns that can interfere in career and relationship success. She is currently writing a series of books on astrology and consciousness.

For more information visit Kerrie's website: www.kerrie-redgate.com

∽

Is it the Body or the Mind that Travels?

KERRIE REDGATE

The longing to reach an exotic destination is not for the food, the entertainment, or the postcards, but a yearning of the soul to complete something undone long ago.

I smiled upwards at the figure standing behind the impossibly high (as I remember it!) podium at the Balinese airport. I handed him my boarding pass for his inspection. A group of uniformed Indonesian armed guards were standing just behind me, their guns secured in their hip holsters. The East Timor Crisis of 1999 was in full swing. My companion, now standing beyond at the railing (several days before his own departure), had considered at the outset of our visit that we had better tell the locals we were British, not Australian. Politics and Travel can be a deadly mix.

The man at the podium focused down at me sharply, his eyebrows drawn together framing his dark eyes. My gosh, what have I done? What is he thinking? We didn't check the morning news! What has happened? He leaned over and held my boarding pass in front of my face. What can be wrong?! My eyes were already dripping tears at having to leave this beautiful island and its spiritually nurturing people grounded in the most practical wisdom.

And then... his eyebrows raised and with the gentlest of smiles, I was caressed with the most sensitive of voices as if I were a little child:

"You have a tear on your boarding pass."

I nearly fainted! "Maaf, maaf," I muttered. Excuse me, I'm sorry.

I smiled and stepped toward the gateway.

Shouts from the armed guards behind me, in unison, like machine-gun fire:

"HEY-HEY, HEY-HEY, HEY-HEY!" Their eyes targeting my own.

I stopped, frozen... my legs feeling like bent pretzels... my heart still and soundless. They all pointed, arms outstretched, at the railing where my companion stood, waving to me. The hardened guards-with-guns all spoke again, but in that gentle Balinese tone:

"Your husband!" Big smiles all around!

Back at Tullamarine Airport in Melbourne, waiting, waiting, for a connecting flight, sympathy and service were thin on the ground! The contrast was like an icy alpine avalanche from nowhere, falling on my head on sunny Bondi Beach.

I have never forgotten the Balinese people, their devotion to their religion and way of life, the surrealism of the place and the natural wisdom so many of them imparted to me… The taxi driver: he found me in tears on the street one morning after my crazed friend had argued me out the door. He had helped me change my flight, even paid for the phone call, and insisted that I could not go back to see my friend right away, "Because the fire is up. You cannot talk to him when the fire is up. You must wait until the fire goes down." Practical wisdom… And the sympathetic shop keeper: a young woman, arms flailing through the air, who made me laugh with "all men, all-world-over, all same!"

But, astoundingly, it was the Balinese airport – cold and sterile and metallic as all airports tend to be – that made the true magic possible. The contrast of such warmth with such sterile efficiency brought the realization, with tears on my cheeks, that all people, all beings, regardless of their personal or professional station in life, regardless of how we accidentally label them, are compassionate at the deepest core. We need never fear anyone if we approach them with kindness and a genuine smile. And conversely, no matter our own station in life, personal or professional, there is *never a moment* when we cannot offer the same compassion and comfort to others.

People will always react to us according to how we treat them, and how we present ourselves. Even if they are insulting or threatening, through showing them respect and acceptance of their own higher nature they will respond in kind. Unlike the American movies that programmed our childhood brains, people cannot be divided into Goodies and Baddies; or Harsh-Authorities and Suffering-Subordinates. Of course we know this; but do we always behave as if we do?

Travel can be stressful, but also enlightening. Perhaps we cannot grasp an enlightened experience without first disarming the fear. Even though we may come to realize that romantic foreign films, travel documentaries, and even news reports, may have misguided our expectations of foreign encounters in other lands, they cannot be wholly blamed for the surprise of the inner reactions we do experience while physically moving through other cultures. Stirred within us are often mysteriously deep chasms of fascination, but not simply for new locations and customs.

The true fascination of travel is with ourselves: with our behavior, attitudes, and even an astonishingly new taste in clothing! We may very often sense the release of being able to express a part of ourselves that was once neglected, dormant, or now shockingly new!

We *feel* different on the inside. Reality shifts. And a vast openness appears, with no boundaries. We are 'catapulted into the World.'

Yes, we are out of our familiar routine. Yes, we are free of the unconscious expectations and projections of many of our friends and colleagues. But is this all that is going on?

The places on this planet that we are drawn to explore are not random or arbitrary places, no matter the mode that got us there in the first place. The soul, the mind-stream, is the memory of our past journeying. The places that move us the most are not necessarily the Power Places like the Acropolis, the Pyramids of Giza, the Vatican of Rome, the Potala Palace of Tibet, Stonehenge, the Delphic Oracle sites of Greece, even the sacred mesas of Arizona and Australia's gigantic sacred rock boulders known as The Olgas. These are places where many people have already left a deeply spiritual impression in antiquity. We cannot help but be impressed by this karmic residue. However, our own Power Places that echo to us the histories that have molded our present form are far greater in effect and may hit the switch of genuine awakening.

Unresolved attachments or, conversely, forgotten greatness (that we have so far not allowed ourselves to touch in this life), can be stirred from the depths of our psyche, from the simplest of places: a small village, a lake's edge, a tiny chapel, even a piece of jewelry in a museum. If we have had connections with such places and objects, our eyes will mist over, and an engaging sense of 'belonging' may flood through us. In some cases, we may even feel the tingling of Goosebumps on our flesh, or the hairs at the back of our neck may prickle. These are all signs of a higher dimension of ourselves trying to break through to the shock of daylight.

Through these signals we can become aware that we are struggling to recall an experience, an important scenario, to which we have been blinded for years, perhaps centuries. And then the Heart opens to receive the experience and reconnect us through threads of time.

Time is a barrier that is manufactured by the mind-stream, the Keeper of Memory. We can no more go back in time than we can reverse gravity, and it would be fruitless to do so. But we can recapture something abandoned, something worth preserving for the benefit of others. Our old skills and greatest moments often sit buried in the mind-stream. Time means nothing to our consciousness. We cannot re-experience the Past, but we can resurrect the best of it in all we do, think and say.

The longing to reach an exotic destination is not for the food, the entertainment, or the postcards, but a yearning of the soul to complete something undone long ago. If we use travel wisely, we can mature as spiritual beings, and find fulfillment in this very life.

For me, Bali was a destination I had been longing to reach for almost four-hundred years, a promise once made by another that could not be fulfilled until 1999… But that's another story!

For as long as I can recall, I had been fascinated by vivid past-life memories that had surfaced in my mind as a child, and which had also been tapped by respected psychic mediums in my early twenties. From a very early age, I had set myself a goal to find the truth behind these memories. And metaphysics aside, there had to be a scientific reason for all this mind-travel, and for our inner stirrings at particular Past-Places. Astrology, I found, provided the perfect tool.

All results have causes, and the astrology chart (the map of the solar system) at birth is a result of something prior. It became obvious to me that our birth chart had to be a collection of the thought-forms we were bringing in with us from the experiences of our previous lives. That idea became the premise of my work and research.

Through the use of thousands of named asteroids, I was excited to find the connections to my past-life memories in my own astrological birth chart. (As one simple example: the asteroid 'Bali' is in a prominent position in my chart, and is astrologically associated with other pertinent asteroids and planets related to the same scenario). These connections were then tested through the use of kinesiology with a gifted colleague interested in past-life investigation. This led to my students and clients also researching their deeper pasts with this combination of tools. All results were astounding!

The naming of asteroids and planets by astronomers has never been incidental, but, rather, highly regarded as a tradition, corresponding with political or personal themes occurring at the time of discovery. The names chosen have been proven to 'resonate' with our experience of the asteroids, astrologically. For decades this has never failed in my own research of applying personal asteroid positions within birth charts.

But how can these memories, these thought-fields, appear in a map of the solar system at birth? It may be that *harmonic resonance* is the principle on which the entire universe is based, at least from our perception of it. And magnetism, a mysterious wonder of the Cosmos, may have more to do with our travel epics than we could ever have suspected.

Memories are thought-fields creating particular vibratory frequencies that impact upon the neural net of the brain. Contrary to the traditional view of Western science, now being questioned, it is the *mind* that creates the *brain*. If this were not the case, meditation practices and serious study would not be able to alter the brain in any way. It is now recognized that the brain is indeed 'plastic', and does continually 'rewire' its neurological structure. However, at the moment of birth, we already have particular areas of brain function available to us. Thought-fields must already have been in place to have developed the brain for our new life. And astonishingly, astrological techniques I have devised are proving that our new life is always built on our old one.

The orbital paths of planets and asteroids around our sun also create inaudible tones of vibratory frequencies, resembling the cycles per second of sound

Fulfillment

*I celebrate the magic
and mystery of life.*

*Just as the full moon brings closure
and release, the end of a journey
brings completion, a time to reflect on
the gifts of the journey behind us.
As we tie up loose ends, preparing
for our next quest, we celebrate the
mystery that life truly has no endings,
only cycles which begin again.*

waves – though, the planetary frequencies are measured as cycles per years or decades. These 'tones' are continually affecting our brain chemistry. Each planet has a frequency that corresponds to a different area of our mind and, hence, body. For example, Mars resonates with kinetic energy, vitality, the drive to achieve goals, the motor cortex, and impacts upon the spleen ch'i; while Mercury resonates with conscious mental energy, language, left-brain processes, and impacts upon lung ch'i.

I had also been led to the work of other researchers such as the astrophysicist, Professor Percy Seymour of Plymouth University in Britain, who delved into the Earth's magnetic field as an explanation for astrological influences.[1]

To put it very simply, the Earth's Magnetic Poles create magnetic field lines stretching from north to south, much like that old science experiment of dropping iron filings onto a sheet of paper hiding a bar magnet beneath, so that the iron filings trace out the north-south lines of magnetic force. The field lines of the Earth behave in the same way and are also much like giant harp strings that are plucked by the solar wind, crushed in on the daytime side of the Earth and simultaneously stretched outward in length on the night-side, as well as the seasonal changes produced by the 23.5° tilt of the Earth on its axis as it rotates while traveling about the sun.

The Earth's field is also affected by the orbital paths of the planets and asteroids, as is the sun itself. This geocentric field resonates with, and constantly alters, our brain chemistry. In fact, it affects the biological processes of all life on this planet (animal, marine, bird, insect, even bacterium). I believe the twelve zodiac signs that are employed in Western Tropical Astrology originate in the frequencies of the Earth's magnetic field, rather than the complex mass of enormously distant star constellations, which were symbolic of what the ancient priests knew as a spiritual phenomenon. Astrology is, indeed, the music of the spheres.

So, how does the Soul or Spirit come into this picture?

Firstly, all things are intrinsically connected. We've heard this before, but what does it mean? *How* are they connected? The idea of Synchronicity, popularized by psychologist Carl Jung, is a *result* not a *cause*. There is something at work behind this, and to begin to understand the process, we need to appreciate the power of *resonance*.

When two tuning forks are designed to produce the same tone (for example, an E note), when placed in close proximity, they will *both* resonate audibly with this tone when only one is struck. Other tuning forks of different tones will not resonate with them.

In the same way, when we are exposed to familiar vibratory frequencies, there is a resonance that occurs within our brain patterning which reproduces the association we had originally formed with those frequencies. This also occurs at the moment of our first breath when we breathe in a symphony of inaudible sound frequencies that resonate with our memories and idea of 'self.' This process ignites particular circuits of association in the brain, hardwiring the effect, which presents our later challenges in life as we make valuable adjustments.

Added to this, even though we are not consciously aware of it, is the strange effect that occurs when we move around the planet and are subjected to the subtle changes in the Earth's magnetic field. Even the distance we travel from the North or South Magnetic Poles can interfere with our usual left or right brain functioning, enhancing or depleting either, according to our natural orientation.[2]

We actually experience other locales as though we had been born there. We still have the same astrology chart, but there is a different emphasis within it. Whereby at home we may deny, for example, the full power of our Mars energy, in another part of the world this planet may be emphasized through the key signature in the Earth's field at that point, unleashing our boldness and daring. Oddly, these sorts of phenomena occur in precisely the places where we had experienced the issue in past times. All things are synchronistic, due to the Resonance principle.

Of course, not all travel experiences are uplifting and joyful. It could be conversely the case, as it was for one of my clients, who experienced Saturn on her Ascendant in a foreign land. For my Australian client, this occurred in a South American country where she was traveling extensively. It took three days for her to be allowed by authorities to cross the border out of the country. It was a highly stressful time. Saturn's frequency can produce challenges to our inner authority and integrity, and may replay old karmic issues for us to finally master.

These sorts of experiences are not random, and not caused expressly by astrological and geomagnetic forces; but these very forces are resonating in a brain that is 'wired' to associate certain frequencies with past experiences. Another person with Saturn on the Ascendant in a foreign land may have a high degree of success in that country, and be *recognized* by others as a figure of authority. It all depends on how we have been using the triggered planets in our life up to this point; and it is our present use of particular planetary frequencies which will lead us to certain foreign lands. The decision to visit those locations will depend on the prevailing thought-forms of memory associated with those planetary frequencies at our birth. All things are subjective. No two persons will see or experience the world in exactly the same way.

My traveling companion in Bali had suffered a violent death there in 1629 as a Dutch trader, and, even though it had occurred four hundred years in the past, this was probably responsible for his trepidation and also choice of timing (the Timor Crisis) in bringing me to that location.

My work with clients has largely focused on uncovering areas of deeply hidden self-sabotage related to past-life persecution of altruistic healing gifts and talents, and a number of my clients have chosen to revisit the exact locations of their former demise, to re-experience the place or culture and, more importantly, to face the resonant terror *and survive it*, thus eliminating the curse of the insidious inner saboteur.

I am happy to report that, despite their worst fears and, in some cases, spontaneous bouts of illness, all of these clients and students survived the process!

Not all past-life travels that accelerate our spiritual growth need be horrendously challenging. There are places we can visit where we had once happily expressed talents that we may simply now need to nurture into completeness for the benefit of many others. These places provide magical inspiration where the challenge is to bring that emotive quality back with us when we arrive home.

A specialist astrologer can determine the challenges and benefits of travel to any area of the planet for any client who has an accurate birth time. This is accomplished through the use of a Relocation Chart which is calculated for the same birth-moment in time, but for the latitude and longitude of the new destination, rather than the birth location.

In my own work, I have collaborated with a number of specialist kinesiologists who have been able to uncover the finer details of past-life experiences pertinent to this life's challenges, always based on the information found in the astrology charts. Sometimes kinesiology provided precise dates of events and previous birth information for my own and my clients' past-life personas. Everything has dovetailed beautifully.

In this way, we can see that it is the Mind, as Soul, that travels. The Mind travels when we are fully conscious of the effect a new location is having on us, when we are aware of the deeper implications of the 'coincidences' we experience in foreign lands, and when we can make sense of these influences and their messages. As with dreaming, the symbolism is guiding us as to a past that is being relived in a habitual psyche that constantly seeks the familiar.

Through travel, we have the opportunity to feel again the people we have been, and the lives we have led. Not for the sake of the ego do we do this. We would not want to cement ourselves into a solid identity. No, that would be a waste. The highest purpose of travel is to reclaim gifts that could now be helpful to many through their integration with our present life and unfolding *beingness*.

And greater yet is to find our own Power Places, to help us resolve or resurrect something lost or buried from within our deepest being. The fascination is indeed with ourselves, with our own spiritual potential, with the many Gifts we had once laid to rest and which could now be helping so many others. It is the Mind that travels. Take it with you next time you step off a plane onto new ground, and rediscover a part of your Spirit that had been missing.

Clues to Discovering your own Power Places

Whether you are preparing to travel to foreign lands, explore your own country, or visit an astrologer to seek the best outcome for your inner or outer journeying, there are clues you can follow to uncover your personal Places of Power before you begin.

Our Soul speaks to us in symbols from the material world that surrounds us. We cloak our world in images from a past we cannot quite remember. The clues are everywhere, ready to explain our most mysterious habits and beliefs, and to inspire our purpose for this incarnation. Other-cultured music and foreign languages may certainly intrigue us, but some of the greatest symbols reflecting your past places can be found within your own home.

As the subconscious mind always seeks security in the familiar, your home, no matter how humble or grandiose, is a vision of your subconscious mind in 3-D. The style of décor you choose often reveals an unresolved lifetime your Soul is yearning to heal or complete. Cabinets from Korea may draw you, rather than similar pieces from China. To the past-life eye, the differences will be easily discernable. You can also combine the influences of your separate passions to discover that an obsession with Spanish antiques may be connected to a love of sailing. These seemingly unrelated interests may combine to recall a sixteenth century Spanish conquistador.

What do you collect? Those little trinkets on your mantle, which are so meaningful to you alone, can be major clues to Past cultures. Do you have ornately gilded mirrors, an old chesterfield couch, or large Dutch painted plates? Look also to the subject matter of those paintings and prints on your walls, and even your shower curtains! One person I knew had an uncommon design of old sailing ships on her shower curtain, and her good friend next door had paintings of old wooden tall ships throughout his house! It is not difficult to imagine where they had known each other before.

There are also fashions and fabrics that can reveal your inner mind: An attraction for puffy sleeves: a European life seeping through? A love of shoulder-padded jackets could be a military influence. Nehru-collared jackets from India, or Indian saris (even as curtains), combined with a love of Indian music, religion, or food, becomes obvious. Fabrics can be descriptive: the distinctive silks from Thailand, batik and ikat from Indonesia, English brocades, European lace, and Andean weaving. Look to the *passion* you feel for these styles rather than purely artistic appreciation.

And jewelry: Special, exotic pieces can often be found in foreign bazaars or hometown market stalls. In fact, antique or culturally-designed jewelry is one of the easiest of clues to our past, such as a strong attraction to Native American jewelry. Such pieces can also have religious significance from the roots of any culture.

Other Places: Museums are fruitful environs of inspiration when you wish to listen to your Soul's longing, as they generally exhibit artifacts from most cultures in antiquity. Browsing local bookstores and libraries can yield unsuspected responses. Reading ancient history can stir the odd emotion: were you on the side of the Athenians or Persians when Darius attacked? Large coffee table publications can be bursting with colorful and inspiring images from your unremembered Pasts. It may not be Egypt so much as a particular Pharaoh that leaps out at you (dating your history to within that Pharaoh's influence). Or are you led to glossy pages on Buddhist temples of Thailand or Cambodia? Or war zones? These fascinations all have a rational source – your own history. Follow the Goosebumps, tears, absorption, or passionate stirrings in your heart.

Films and novels: Write a list of all your favorite films and novels, and look for the common themes. Is it the locations, time periods, politics, or similar stories that are areas of intrigue for you? Repetitive story themes are usually highly significant in explaining your own past scenarios.

Another important aspect of 'soul travel' is in becoming aware of the clues from your children regarding their own previous lives, as children under the age of seven are highly influenced, emotionally, by their former existence. I once witnessed a dyslexic child of six years instantly cured of his insistence on reading words backwards. After considering his unusual gift of being able to discern the subtle differences between Chinese and Japanese music, it became obvious to me that his 'dyslexia' was coming from an immediately prior life in China. He had been told up to this point that it is *wrong* to read or write from right to left. Of course, he disregarded such nonsense as he had probably been doing just that, quite effectively, in China for a good seventy years! In circumstances like this, it becomes necessary to *re-language* our instruction: "In *this* country, we read and write from left to right." This allows for change to occur.

Denial of our Past is not Wisdom; yet dwelling too much on our Past without making use of it in the Present is also not Wisdom. If we find we are passionately drawn to a particular style from another culture, or even a past style from our own culture, it is a sign that this is the time to reclaim what had been lost there.

Travel is certainly one powerful way of doing this. But as it is the Mind, ultimately, that travels, our spiritual insights and deep inner searching can occur absolutely anywhere, even on our very own couch.

☙

1,2 Even though the Earth's Magnetic Poles are weak compared to the many electromagnetic fields in our immediate environment, it is the Magnetic Poles' frequency of resonance that is significant for us. See Dr John Diamond and his research with magnets and the human brain through kinesiology in his book *Your Body Doesn't Lie*, Grand Central Publishing, New York, 1989.

Bibliography

Dr Percy Seymour, *Astrology: The Evidence of Science*, Arkana/Penguin, London, 1990.

SOPHIA FAIRCHILD

Sydney, Australia

SOPHIA FAIRCHILD is an award-winning editor and publisher, professional soul mentor and author who lives beside the whale migration routes on Sydney's north coast.

Sophia grew up around Australian aboriginal people, saw faeries and spoke to angelic spirits as a child. Her Irish great aunts and Aboriginal great grandfather have profoundly influenced her playfulness, intuitive gifts and love of storytelling.

Her stories have appeared widely in publication, including *Soul Moments*, also published as *Coincidence or Destiny*, edited by Phil Cousineau, foreword by Robert A. Johnson, Conari Press, 1997; *Traveler's Tales: Tuscany*, Traveler's Tales Guides, 2001; *Angels 101*, by Doreen Virtue, Hay House, 2006; *Angel on My Shoulder*, Malachite Press, 2007; *The Miracles of Archangel Michael*, by Doreen Virtue, Hay House, 2008; *Soul Whispers: Collective Wisdom from Soul Coaches around the World*, Soul Wings® Press, 2009; *The Healing Miracles of Archangel Raphael*, by Doreen Virtue, Hay House, 2010; *Soul Whispers II: Secret Alchemy of the Elements in Soul Coaching,* Soul Wings® Press, 2011 (Gold Medal Winner for *Spirit Book of the Year* – Living Now Book Awards), *Angels: Winged Whispers – True Stories from Angel Experts around the World*, Soul Wings® Press, 2011, and *The Wisdom We Have Gained,* edited by Kim Pentecost.

Look for award-winning books edited by Sophia Fairchild, available worldwide.

For editing and publishing services contact her at Soul Wings® Press.
www.SoulWingsPress.com

∽

Souvenirs

SOPHIA FAIRCHILD

We were camped in the shadow of Uluru,
the most sacred site in the heart of Australia.

I must have dozed off briefly, waking up with a start around midnight in the middle of the desert. I opened my eyes and glanced up at the night sky. Stretched out above, the constellations of the Southern Cross, Orion's Belt and the Seven Sisters (the Pleiades) were all pulsating with blazing intensity. From horizon to horizon, this brilliant canopy of dazzling stars was so alive it was almost frightening.

An enormous, tangible, starry presence dwarfed me. It was as if the Universe, the whole of outer space was pressing down, piercing through the veil of earth's atmosphere, to reach down and pluck me from the curved surface of the planet, scooping me up into a whirlpool of swirling galaxies and dreaming stars.

I glanced toward the campfire. In the flickering firelight, old women from two clan groups were still singing and dancing long Dreamtime stories to each other, and to the land and stars above. Then the earth seemed to crumble away beneath my body and I found myself suspended in a sea of stars, along with the chanting women, all bound up together inside the vortex of the secret Dreamtime story of this magical place, and these infinite stars.

We were camped in the shadow of Uluru, the most sacred site in the heart of Australia. What I had just glimpsed was a fraction of the concentrated power of the Dreaming in this place. I understood in an instant what the mythologist Joseph Campbell had meant when he said that to see the face of the Divine can be a sublime and terrifying experience. Beholding the starry dome of heaven in this hallowed place, I felt as if I had indeed stared directly into the face of the Creator. I closed my eyes in reverence.

I awoke again as the pink halo of dawn silhouetted the dark shape of the sacred rock against a cloudless sky. One lone star, a blinking Venus, hung low above the indigo horizon, reminding me of the revelry of dancing stars I had entered into overnight. The aromas of wood smoke, pungent desert herbs and rich, red dust filled my nostrils. The presence of the sacred monolith, Uluru, now glowing violet, two miles wide and towering 1,000 feet above everything else, dominated the flat desert landscape for as far as the eye could see.

The two youngest aboriginal girls were now awake, sitting up in their blankets rubbing the sleep from their eyes. All the older women were still asleep in their swags, circled around the pink ashes of last night's campfire. The little girls smiled silently at me as the three of us crept out of our camp beds, signaling to each other in sign language so as not to disturb our elders.

I filled the metal billycan with water from our small supply, then carefully placed it into the glowing embers. Pulling on a sweater, I joined the two little girls as they set out to scout for perentie tracks, taking up where we'd left the playful hunt at nightfall yesterday. This large totemic goanna, the 'painted perentie,' is featured in Central Australian Dreaming stories and ceremonies, and provides important bush medicine for the desert people.

We immediately noticed that a large wild dog had circled our camp during the night. Fat dingo footprints punctuated the fine red desert sand, telling the vivid story of its silent reconnaissance of our campsite under cover of darkness, before turning back in the direction of the great red rock. *Was he hunting us or blessing us?* The little girls giggled noiselessly with excitement as we set out to follow the story of these dingo tracks, away from the sleeping camp.

I looked back over my shoulder to check that the billycan was still sitting upright on the remains of the fire, and noticed that my friend and sister, Panaji, was now awake. We smiled to each other in recognition of our shared joy in waking up to the pristine beauty of this sacred place. She lay back down in her swag to shelter from the dawn chill, while I led the two little girls off into the desert, following the dingo tracks and looking for fuel for the fire. The older women would be needing some strong billy tea when they awoke from their long night of dancing the Dreaming stories, in honor of this place.

I took no photos during this part of my journey. The memory of those fat dingo footprints in the soft, red sand leading us towards the huge sacred rock, which rose from the heart of the desert like a giant amethyst against a rosy dawn, is etched in my memory forever. These, and the midnight vision of the symphony of sacred stars, dancing across the dreaming night sky as the old women sang, were the only souvenirs I would ever need.

I often wonder if our presence in that place also became the souvenired memories of the wild dingo, the painted perentie, or the sacred rock…

Sometimes the old white bushman or aborigine 'just sits'
but sometimes he 'just sits and thinks,'
and to the latter at least, the thinking may include receiving,
and for the man of high degree (i.e., the shaman)
it may include 'sending messages on the wind.'

—A. P. ELKIN

Why is it that we humans feel the need to collect things from nature in the form of souvenirs?

Every natural history museum in the world is filled with enormous collections of things like dinosaur bones, mineral and zoological specimens and everything from ancient artifacts to space rocks. This is seen as preserving our past history for the public good. But why do we collect souvenirs as individuals? People everywhere have made a hobby of collecting anything from artworks and sea shells to teddy bears, baseball cards and precious stones.

The original private collectors were wealthy aristocrats, for whom their souvenirs served as a way of displaying their social status, sometimes ensuring fame. Yet one thing all professional collectors have in common is that their collections are never quite complete. It seems there is always an even more prized piece to be hunted down and added to the private cache.

Modern psychology explains this act of acquiring collections as providing a sense of emotional security, a way to fill a void in the personal sense of self. Collectors also derive great pleasure from rearranging their collections. This ability to order and classify objects offers a soothing sense of control over larger unknown factors in life. Thus, collections can become a form or insurance against private feelings of loss or uncertainty.

Most people would agree there is a painful abnormality in the personal lives of chronic hoarders, people whose lives have been overtaken by a need to collect too much of everything. And depression is a common symptom among those who suffer from both compulsive shopping and hoarding – behaviors which also serve as coping mechanisms for feelings of overwhelming anxiety and a sense of lack.

But of course, the little keep-sakes that you and I collect and treasure are much more likely to be a way for us to relive and remember some cherished moment from the past. Spending time with our treasures allows us to smile and be briefly transported to that soft other-world of blissful memories.

In the past, archeologists, amateur explorers and students of medical science have collected sacred artifacts and even human remains from numerous 'primitive cultures' to take home and study. This 'finders keepers' mentality over such sacred material has in recent years become the subject of legal claims. Various indigenous peoples including Native Americans, Maoris and Australian Aborigines, have demanded that the remains of their ancestors, housed in foreign museums, be returned for ceremonial burial in the lands of their origin. These and other sacred artifacts, correctly perceived as stolen, have in a number of cases been successfully repatriated.

> *It should be said at once that the completely profane world,*
> *the wholly desacralized cosmos, is a recent discovery*
> *in the history of the human spirit.*

—MIRCEA ELIADE

The outlawed spiritual warrior, Jandamarra, was a freedom-fighter from the Kimberly region of Western Australia who resisted white pastoralists when they scattered his people, preventing them from accessing their country for food and ceremony. Drawing his legendary mystical powers from a strong relationship with his ancestral lands, Jandamurra eluded the constant pursuit of the authorities for six years. His passionate resistance was motivated by deep spiritual connections to both his sacred lands and the creator snake, to heal and protect the spirit of his country and his people. In 1897, Jandamurra's trophied head was sent to London for the private collection of a gun manufacturer. It is still missing.

In other cases, no legal action has been necessary to achieve the return of stolen objects to their rightful place. The United States Park Service in Hawaii Volcanoes National Park regularly receives packages of black sand and lava rock, taken as souvenirs by visitors. Some say they are returning the items out of respect for the Goddess Pele, while others believe that removing the rocks has resulted in personal bad luck.

Similarly, every day of the year, the Uluru-Kata Tjuta National park in Central Australia receives parcels of souvenired rocks and sand, returned from around the world by past visitors to Ayers Rock, usually accompanied by hand-written notes of apology.

These parcels may also contain seeds, twigs, seashells, and even photographs of sacred sites, giving the park rangers the complicated task of determining the exact origins of each item. The volume of returned rocks increased dramatically after these sacred lands were handed back to their traditional owners by the Australian Government in 1985. Some of these souvenirs were collected up to 40 years ago and rocks have been returning in a steady daily stream from countries all over the world since the late 1970s.

All must pass through quarantine treatment before making their way back into the desert heart of Australia. Scientific analysis reveals that these 'sorry rocks,' as they are termed, originate from many different parts of the vast national park, and some are not even Australian in origin. For the past decade, all of the returned rocks, along with their accompanying letters, have been kept in a permanent collection at the site.

But why are these souvenirs being returned in such vast numbers? In one way, it demonstrates our insatiable human desire to collect things that remind us of a particular place, to 'capture the magic' so to speak. So strong is this desire to own a personal connection with a special place, that people risk stealing these items in spite of the threat of huge fines, in this case $5,000 for illegal removal of rocks, soil or sand from Uluru. But this is not the reason these 'little pieces of place' are being returned.

The sorry rocks are given back out of fear and guilt. Personal notes sent anonymously with the rocks, one weighing 75 pounds, carry messages such as "Many years ago our family visited Uluru and collected these pieces of rock. We have had pangs of guilt ever since. Could you please return them to their rightful place?" One tourist wrote "This rock has been longing for return. Today it has broken into two and made its final request to return to its source." Others speak of experiencing ill health, feeling cursed or having bad luck. All express contrition and a wish to see these pieces of Uluru returned home.

The Anangu people of Uluru-Kata Tjuta consider this site holy. And although their *tjukurpa*, or ancient Dreaming Law, holds that there are consequences for disobeying the law of the land, they say there is no curse connected with these rocks. They suggest that people who take fragments of Uluru shouldn't blame the rock, but instead look within. They are very grateful when visitors share their respect for the land, and acknowledge these returned rocks as a sign of this respect. However, they believe the rocks and sand belong at Uluru, and not in the homes of visitors. They ask, "Please, please, don't take any more. Don't take anything from Uluru. It's fine to take a photo home… but leave the rocks."

Aboriginal people have been living around this sacred mountain in the heart of Australia for at least 22,000 years. Seasonal ceremonies and rock paintings in surrounding caves have kept the sacred Dreaming alive here for millennia, just as the waterholes around its sandstone base have sustained life in this harsh desert country for animals, plants and humans alike. It's a place where the ancestors still live. So sacred is Uluru to the aboriginal people, that if a returned rock was originally souvenired from the summit of Uluru, the traditional owners and Park Rangers are prevented by ancient aboriginal law from climbing the monolith to return the sorry rock to its source. The power of the Dreaming is strong here.

But what is *the Dreaming*?

The Dreaming, commonly termed the *Dreamtime*, is both that time when the Ancestors walked the land creating the world, and also the present time. When it comes to the Dreaming, the aboriginal concept of time is a combination of the past, present and future. All time is now. Therefore, everything that was created in the Dreamtime must be continually created now and into the future, to maintain its existence. This is achieved by performing specific ceremonies that were given to the people by the Ancestor Spirits.

Dreaming Stories travel across the landscape as songlines, along which the Creator Ancestors once traveled, bringing everything into being. The Dreamings provide the necessary links of relationship between the people and the land, stretching out into a vast web of stories and songs, held together like constellations of stars strewn out across our galaxy.

If we can understand that in the Dreamtime, all time is now, then from this present moment, we are able to extend our experience of time all the way back to the beginning of Creation. From there, we are able to get a sense that all that occurred in ancient times is also progressing forward towards us to where we are sitting right now – and beyond us – towards an infinite future, where all possibilities and potentials exist, awaiting manifestation and experience.

This law... this country... this people... No matter what people...
Red, yellow, black, or white... the blood is the same.
Lingo little bit different... But no matter.
Country... you in other place, but same feeling.
Blood... bone... all the same.

—BILL NEIDJIE, GAGUDJU BUNITJ ELDER

When I first met the Aboriginal Women, I was given a *skin-sister* name, so that as we traveled together when they took me hunting, I would have a defined place within the extended family group. A skin name, like a kin name, defines one's status, role and relationships within a complex tribal group. By bestowing a sister-name on me, I could be more easily assimilated into the culture of the group. It enabled me to participate more fully in the day to day work activities of the camp, and to become deeply immersed in the world of a female Aboriginal family group, traveling together in the desert.

Though I have aboriginal blood and grew up around Aboriginal people, I still wasn't fully prepared for the total immersion in Aboriginal culture that traveling in the Central Australian desert called for. Survival of the group in the desert wilderness requires order and vigilance regarding the sharing of resources. It also requires a lot of cooperative effort to collect and manage them. All knowledge must be earned over a period of many years and it is a violation of the Laws of the Dreaming for its caretakers to reveal specific cultural secrets. Such transgressions are always subject to serious consequences, because ultimately, they diminish the Dreaming itself.

Long before white settlement, different clan groups were responsible, as a collection of skin groups, for all of the lands and Dreamings within their tribal reach. And much of this wild country still lies beyond the reach of man-made dirt roads. Each section of land belongs to a specific Dreaming story, ceremony and song, and the Dreaming belongs to the people who are its caretakers. This entire continent has been sung continuously for around 40,000 years.

...the aborigines have made the 'face of the Earth' their Bhagavad
Gita, their Tora, their Bible, or Koran. Indeed the Dreaming is the
Aboriginal Ark of the Covenant, which they have been carrying about
the Australian continent since the beginning of time.

—JAMES COWAN, IN *Speaking for the Earth*

To this day, most people know very little about aboriginal 'women's business' (secret ceremonial activity) and even less has been documented. In 1943, when Professor Elkin wrote his book *Aboriginal Men of High Degree* about shamanism in aboriginal culture, he would not have been invited to witness women's private ceremony or to interview them about their secret spiritual practices. Most of the early anthropologists and researchers were male, and thus were not allowed inside the secret world of aboriginal women due to strict cultural taboos.

Therefore, for a long time it was wrongly assumed that aboriginal women had no spiritual authority, and that shamanism was the exclusive domain of the karadji men. Nothing could be further from the truth. However, this widely held misconception allowed aboriginal women to continue on with their sacred practices, as they always had, as if they were invisible.

Even today, traditional Aboriginal people speak up to five languages – their own tribal language, plus several surrounding aboriginal dialects and variations. The English they speak, if any, is usually a form of Aboriginal-English, which is not the same as the Standard English tongue. Historically, this language barrier has prevented the outside world from understanding the nuances and complexities of traditional aboriginal life.

Not only was there no written language text to describe the full extent of their ceremonies, but traditional aboriginal people also employ a complex and extensive sign language – especially during ritual times – when the business of the Dreaming is so powerful that it is considered too dangerous to speak of it aloud. This means that strangers have had very little chance of ever decoding the secrets of women's business.

The Law of the Dreaming is highly valued by those still living in the traditional way, and few would survive even the shame of breaking this Law. This is why the Dreaming remains both strong and secret, in those places where it is maintained, especially for the women.

The Aboriginal grandmothers, aunties, sisters and daughters all taught me a great deal about how they still manage their lands, and their Dreamings, holding them sacred for all of time. This is a priceless gift for me, but a far more valuable treasure for the two little girls who smiled quietly as we followed those dingo tracks into the desert dawn.

> *If God created the earth,*
> *so is the earth hallowed;*
> *and if it is hallowed,*
> *so must we deal with it devotedly*
> *and with care that we do not despoil it,*
> *and be mindful of our relations to all beings that live on it.*
> *We are to consider it religiously:*
> *Put off thy shoes from they feet,*
> *for whereon thou standest is holy ground.*

> —L. H. BAILEY

Indigenous spirituality worldwide is based on the idea that the Creator Spirit lives within everything – the rocks, the water, the wind and fire. It is difficult for people who hold such beliefs to understand why anyone would want to steal souvenirs from the earth, since they are everywhere, freely available for everyone to see and experience.

We too can honor the sacredness of the created world, as well as our interconnectedness with everything in nature. By doing so, we become aware that we are both part of creation and co-creators of it. And in our roles as co-creators, we also have the power to destroy. The choice is ours.

When we 'take' things from Mother Earth as souvenirs, especially if it is to fill a perceived inner need or feeling of lack, we are affirming our separateness from the Earth. By contrast, in the act of recognizing the divine presence within all created things, we are affirming and restoring the sacredness of the natural world.

New Day

Though life transforms,
the essence remains unchanged.

With ancestral roots eternally stable
within the earth, our spirit explores
new dimensions. Like a butterfly
emerging from its cocoon, we trust in
the enduring power of transformation.
The ancestors light the way as we
breathe new life into our world,
created anew with the birth
of each new day.

Next time you stoop to pick up a souvenir from anywhere in nature, ask yourself if it's really necessary to take this item away from where you found it. Certain shells on the beach, for example, are reusable homes for tiny sea creatures. If we take these shells home to admire, they may look pretty amongst our possessions for a time, but may eventually end up being discarded, far from their original home, having lost their intended purpose. Perhaps they might be better left on the beach.

Do we really need to collect souvenirs from the Earth? And do these objects wish to be taken? You will hear the answers and know what is right for you to do if you approach these questions with your full awareness. If for some reason it is vitally important for you to take a gift from the land, perhaps you can reciprocate this action with an appropriate energy exchange. Is there some other way you can honor and give back to the land?

One alternative to taking home a souvenir is to hold the treasured item in your hands; honor it for what it represents for you, and infuse it with love and a blessing. Listen for the message it holds for your spirit. You may embrace this moment of awareness, and the object, for as long as you wish, in order to capture this memory. Then replace the item back where you found it.

Mother Earth will surely thank us for such kindness.

Bliss Balls

Instead of loving our Planet Earth to death by taking pieces of her as souvenirs, what can we do instead to give something of value back?

Environmental disturbances on our planet often involve things that have become problematic because they're 'out of place'. These may be naturally occurring substances such as minerals or chemicals that only begin to create imbalances in ecosystems after we've relocated them or removed them from where they once existed naturally.

Fortunately, nature has the ability to clean, purify and rebalance water, land and air over time through the power of the sun and weather, along with all of the natural processes that take place during the life cycles of living organisms – such as trees and plants, and all the living species of the air, sea and earth, plus a multitude of hard working invisible microorganisms.

Around any urban environment you'll find vacant lots, abandoned construction sites and other areas of barren, compacted soil where the natural vegetation has been removed or disturbed by some form of human activity.

Bliss Balls (also known as Seed Balls or Earth Dumplings) are a very effective way of re-vegetating such degraded areas of land, allowing these sites to be naturally restored. The modern use of Seed Balls, originally utilized by First Nation peoples, was developed by Japanese ecologist Fukuoka Masanobu as a no-till method of environmental restoration through re-vegetation.

Bliss Balls can be used not only for native habitat restoration, erosion control and grey water filtration, but also for growing wildflowers and edible plants. They create a protected environment for seed distribution, preventing seeds from drying out, or being blown away or eaten by insects or animals whilst they germinate. Bliss Balls are especially effective for sites where rainfall is unpredictable.

Seed selection should be carefully considered. If planting non-native seeds, like vegetables, it's best to distribute these near residential housing or in urban areas. For everywhere else, it's important to select seeds of plants that are indigenous to that particular area, for example, native wildflowers.

Bliss Ball Recipe

- One part heritage seeds (use a combination of seeds of plants that are known to support each other and grow well together)
- Three parts dry organic compost (not animal manure)
- Five parts organic clay (brown or red clay is best; use local where possible)
- Water, as needed (enough to allow the mixture to stick together)
- Mix clay and compost together, removing any rocks or large clumps.

- Spread a layer of this mixture out and sprinkle your seed mixture on top.

- Add enough water to make the mixture sticky.

- Roll this mud mixture into balls about the size of a marble.

- Infuse them with love.

- Allow your Bliss Balls to dry in a shady place for a few days. Avoid storing in plastic.

- When dry, scatter at the rate of one Bliss Ball per square foot or 10 per square meter.

- Distribute these at any time of the year, or store them for planting in the spring. Your seeds will germinate when the rains come, nourished by nutrients and microbes in their clay shell. This method of planting requires no plowing, no weeding, no fertilizer and no biocides.

Bliss Balls are a thoughtful way of giving something of value back to Planet Earth.

Connection

*All is energetically connected to the
healing power of Mother Earth.*

*Our ancestors found balance and joy
through honoring Earth Mother with
seasonal ceremony. By seeking our
own balanced center, we learn how to
bend with the wind, allowing natural
forces to show us the way, finding
compassion, contentment
and connection with all.*

Blessing

We wish you many blessings as you listen for your own planet whispers…

May you be blessed by
Heaven's strength
Sun's light
Moon's radiance
Fire's splendor
Lightning's speed
Wind's swiftness
Ocean's depth
Earth's stability
Rock's firmness
Ancestors' wisdom.
May you be blessed.

Adapted from the Old Celtic *Faeth Fiada,*
reprinted in *Liber Hymnorum*, Bernard & Atkinson, Dublin, 1898
and *Fíanaigecht*, Kuno Meyer, Dublin, 1910.

Acknowledgements

Immense gratitude goes to each of the remarkable Soul Travelers who've shared their stories and insights throughout the pages of this book. Your wisdom provides us all with a truly inspirational and evocative guide for listening to the whispers of our planet.

Many thanks go to Fiona Raven for crafting the design of these magical pages. Thank you also to the authors' loved ones for supporting them on their journey. Finally, we offer deep gratitude to those who came before us, our ancestors, and to those who are yet to come, for guiding the birth of this book with infinite grace and love.

"In this very special book, you will be amazed at the variety of ways the authors have shared their personal life-changing *Planet Whispers*. For some, it was through visiting a sacred site such as Machu Picchu in Peru, while for others it was being in a common place or connecting with a simple object or piece of jewelry. For another, it was feeling a push to go to a destination without really knowing exactly why, to find himself experiencing a profound vision quest in the isolation and solitude of the Yukon in the Canadian wilderness. As you enjoy these captivating stories of real life people sharing thought-provoking inspiration and insight, perhaps you too will begin to recognize your own *Planet Whispers*!"

—CINDY EYLER, Author of "Dead People in My Life"
Founder of Light Activation Healing System® and
Spiritual and Transformational Journey Leader
www.HealingYourSoul.com   www.Traveling4Life.com

About Soul Wings® Press

Publishing for the Soul®

Soul Wings® Press is an award-winning Small Press Publisher.
We specialize in providing compassionate, professional editorial services
and quality book publishing to assist experts in the fields of
Spirituality and Self-help to become published authors.

If you wish to read interviews with our authors,
or become an author yourself, please visit our website.
www.SoulWingsPress.com

Soul Wings® Press Titles
of related Interest

Soul Whispers: Collective Wisdom from Soul Coaches around the World ©2009
Soul Whispers II: Secret Alchemy of the Elements in Soul Coaching ©2011
Angels: Winged Whispers–True Stories from Angel Experts around the World ©2011

Soul Wings® Press
Publishing for the Soul®
668 N Coast Hwy, Suite 234
Laguna Beach CA 92651 USA
125 Oxford Street, Suite 125
Bondi Junction NSW 2022 Australia
www.SoulWingsPress.com

www.ingramcontent.com/pod-product-compliance
Lightning Source LLC
Chambersburg PA
CBHW071446090426
42737CB00011B/1796